The *Social Sciences*
Their Nature and Uses

The Paul V. Harper Memorial Fund
has been of great help in meeting
the expenses of the Symposium and this publication.
That help is acknowledged
with appreciation.

William H. Kruskal, *Editor*

The Social Sciences
Their Nature and Uses

Papers Presented at the
50th Anniversary of the
Social Science Research Building,
the University of Chicago,
December 16–18, 1979

The University of Chicago Press

Chicago and London

The University of Chicago Press, Chicago 60637
The University of Chicago Press, Ltd., London

©1982 by The University of Chicago
All rights reserved. Published 1982
Printed in the United States of America
89 88 87 86   5 4 3 2

Library of Congress Cataloging in Publication Data

The Social sciences, their nature and uses.

   Sponsored by the University of Chicago, Division
of the Social Sciences.
   Includes bibliographical references.
   Contents: Are social problems problems that
social science can solve? / Herbert A. Simon —
Effects of credentials, connections, and competence
   on income / Paul E. Peterson — Individual experi-
   ence and cultural order / Marshall Sahlins —
   [etc.]
     1. Social sciences—Congresses. I. Kruskal,
William, 1919– II. University of Chicago.
Division of the Social Sciences.
H22.S73   300   81–16263
ISBN 0–226–45499–1   AACR2

Contents

Honorary Degrees Awarded at the Convocation Celebrating the Fiftieth Anniversary of the Social Science Research Building December 18, 1979

Philip E. Converse, Robert Cooley Angell Distinguished College Professor of Sociology and Political Science, University of Michigan

Lee J. Cronbach, Vida Jacks Professor of Education, Stanford University

Otis Dudley Duncan, Professor of Sociology, University of Arizona

Clifford Geertz, Professor of Social Science, Institute for Advanced Study, Princeton University

Erving Goffman, Benjamin Franklin Professor of Anthropology and Sociology, University of Pennsylvania

Lawrence Stone, Dodge Professor of History and Director of the Davis Center for Historical Research, Princeton University

Jean-Pierre Vernant, Professor of Comparative Ancient Religion, College de France

William S. Vickrey, McVickar Professor of Political Economy, Columbia University

Faculty Committee for the Fiftieth Anniversary of the Social Science Research Building

Robert McC. Adams, Dean, Division of the Social Sciences; Harold H. Swift Distinguished Service Professor, Oriental Institute and Departments of Anthropology and Near Eastern Languages and Civilizations; Director, Oriental Institute

James S. Coleman, University Professor, Departments of Sociology and Education, School of Social Service Administration; Committee on Public Policy Studies

Norton S. Ginsburg, Professor and Chairman, Department of Geography

Chauncy D. Harris, Samuel N. Harper Distinguished Service Professor, Department of Geography; Director, Center for International Studies

Neil Harris, Professor, Department of History

William H. Kruskal, Dean, Division of the Social Sciences; Ernest DeWitt Burton Distinguished Service Professor, Department of Statistics

C. Ranlet Lincoln, Dean, University Extension; Associate Professor New Collegiate Division

Bernice L. Neugarten, Professor Emeritus, Department of Behavioral Sciences

Robert Rosenthal, Curator, Department of Special Collections, University Libraries

Theodore W. Schultz, Charles L. Hutchinson Distinguished Service Professor Emeritus, Department of Economics

Academic titles, connections, and responsibilities inevitably vary with time; in particular, the committee members have had somewhat changing roles over the period from anniversary planning, through the celebration itself, to the current 1982 publication. With a few exceptions, however, the identifications above are at the time of the 1979 anniversary. Recent deanships of the Division might be clarified for the sake of future academic historians: Professor Adams served as Dean for the four academic years 1970–71 through 1973–74, and again for the year 1979–80; Professor Kruskal was Dean for the five years 1974–75 through 1978–79, and is at publication time serving for a second term that began with 1980–81.

Introduction

William H. Kruskal

UNIVERSITY OF CHICAGO

The Social Science Research Building at the University of Chicago was dedicated in December 1929, amid high hopes for wider and deeper understanding of human society by means of freshly vigorous research in the social sciences. Funds for construction of the building came from the Laura Spelman Rockefeller Memorial Fund, a precursor of the Rockefeller Foundation.

The dedication was accompanied by scholarly lectures and discussions, brought together in the volume *The New Social Science,* under the editorship of Leonard D. White. Ten years later Louis Wirth organized a celebration of the first decade, and its proceedings appeared under the title *Eleven Twenty-six: A Decade of Social Science Research.* The tradition continued for the building's twenty-fifth anniversary in 1954; the papers of that celebration were published as *The State of the Social Sciences* under the editorship of Professor White. All three volumes were published by the University of Chicago Press.

The form, function, and content of such academic ceremonial occasions might provide excellent study material for a Martian anthropologist studying our subcultural ways. Similarly, the materials in the three publications could lead to a fascinating content analysis by social scientists here or elsewhere. Such themes, however, are perhaps better left to future social and intellectual historians who may be in a readier position to judge the long arc of growth and change of the social sciences.

With the approach of the building's fiftieth anniversary, it became clear again that an appropriate next celebration should be held, and that it should celebrate scholarship by some form of self-exemplification: seminars, lectures, discussions. One approach might, for example, lavish attention and praise on the superb research achievements carried out by members of the division during the prior twenty-five years, for example, T. W. Schultz's analyses of human capital, or Jacob Getzels's study of creativity, or Leo Goodman's new methods of statistical analysis applied to social mobility tables, or . . . The attempt to draw up a list shows the difficulty. So much has been done that one could not begin to cover it with even rough balance.

Another approach would be examination of broad changes in the social sciences over the last fifty years. That itself would be a major piece of social science research, and one made difficult by major differences among the social sciences in terms of viewpoint, self-confidence, methodology, and recent history.

It then seemed to the planning committee desirable to treat the social sciences as they interact with society; in particular, the committee felt that the mutual influences of social science research and the determination and execution of social policy would form a fine central theme. Thus many of the papers in this volume are about, or relate to, the use of social science research in the formation and carrying out of broad policy decisions.

As if to form a continuing self-exemplifying drama, a number of divisional faculty members complained about that theme. "Too narrow," they said, "and too utilitarian. We should have more in the program that celebrates basic social science research by exhibiting it." And so some of the papers are primarily surveys of social science topics, or exemplary pieces of social science research, or—of course—both together.

Three papers, then, illustrate or explain—in their interestingly individual ways—research in three parts of the social sciences. To begin with, Paul E. Peterson's "Effects of Credentials, Connections, and Competence on Income" exhibits a thoroughly quantitative approach to a question of great social importance: What are the determiners of individual income? Peterson describes a survey (and its analysis) in which are measured the apparent effects upon income of family socio-economic class, education, and verbal ability. It turns out for the white population studied that verbal ability and education have the greatest effect on income. In contrast with earlier studies, family socioeconomic class has only a weak effect on income, a relevant finding for discussions of equality and opportunity. Peterson ends his paper by pointing at its connections to the self-confidence of social scientists and to the opposite pressures from social criticism coming from the right and left wings of the political spectrum.

Marshall D. Sahlins's paper, "Individual Experience and Cultural Order," contrasts in many ways with Peterson's. Where Peterson is quantitative, cool, and specific, Sahlins is qualitative and impressionistic, sardonic and witty, allusive and broad. He presents a critical review of the idea that culture is a superorganic object, independent of the humans who enact it. Along with that review, Sahlins—in further contrast with Peterson—treats the dominant utilitarianism of our own culture with something of the skeptical dispassion that the hypothetical Martian anthropologist might show.

In still a third mode, Mary Jean Bowman provides an essay on a theme that cuts across the social sciences: time and its uses. In her paper, "Choice in the Spending of Time," Professor Bowman points out likenesses between time and money (we spend both), but emphasizes that the way we spend our time is the more fundamental. Synchronization of activities in time becomes increasingly complex and formalized with economic development: punctuality and the time discipline of coordinated industrial activity are learned gradually. Marshall's concepts of the long run and the short run are used in modified form to analyze "free time" and its relationship to the time horizons of choices. The rising value of "market time" (i.e., paid-for time) has profound effects on the spending of time with and by children and old people. This has major implications for future markets and future public policies.

These three[1] varied descriptions of social science research all deal with topics having major connections with social policymaking, governmental or private. Yet they do not focus on those connections, nor do the connections appear as primary motivations. In the next set of papers, by contrast, connections between the social sciences and social policy are on center stage. (That the papers are at the same time pieces of social science analysis is worth noting.)

The magisterial address by Herbert A. Simon directly sets out in its title a basic question, "Are Social Problems Problems That

1. A fourth paper would be described here were its publication not preempted by prior commitments. It was given by Lawrence Stone and titled "The Revival of Narrative: Reflections on a New-Old History."

Social Science Can Solve?'' Professor Simon's answer is in parts: Yes, for relatively specific problems, like compensatory education and organizational decision making. But for the great, inescapable problems—War, Poverty, Disease—the social sciences, now and in the foreseeable future, will not have much by way of solutions. The contributions rather will be in terms of deeper understandings. A pervasive difficulty is that of unexpected consequences of a solution to an apparently limited part of a problem.

Lee J. Cronbach takes a far more skeptical position in his "Prudent Aspirations for Social Inquiry." He admonishes us not to dream of rationalist social sciences that somehow mimic the natural sciences. In the social sciences, Cronbach points out, we can rarely do experiments under realistic conditions—or under broad sets of conditions. We are all thoroughly imbued with our cultures, and that hinders generalizations; so we have a link with Sahlin's paper. The role of the social scientist, says Cronbach, is primarily to develop concepts and to ask hard questions, thus he seems to agree with Simon's position . . . but Cronbach applies to all the social sciences the limited role that Simon describes as we confront the monstrous, apocalyptic issues.

Philip E. Converse, in his written discussion, disagrees sharply with Professor Cronbach. Converse believes, first, that Cronbach's skepticism stems from an early overoptimism; second, that in many ways the social sciences may hope to achieve sharp, general results; and, third, that there are large parts of the natural sciences that are themselves still, as Converse puts it, "waiting for Newton."

A constructive view is also taken by James S. Coleman, in his contribution, presented as the address of the University of Chicago's autumn convocation, "Policy, Research, and Political Theory," Professor Coleman describes the increasingly important field of social policy research, how it is carried out in a variety of settings (usually either in universities or in private research firms), and how its quality needs careful, constant attention.

Barry D. Karl traces the history of public and private support of academic research in America. His paper, "The Citizen and the Scholar: Ships That Crash in the Night," describes four models for that support in terms of the writings of four famous social scientists of recent past generations: (1) Thorstein Veblen regarded scientists as the engineers and managers of society; (2) Harold Laski, on the contrary, argued for the importance of the isolated intellectual and against outside funding or the idea of organized team research; (3) a priestly role, celebrating the donor's merits, was stressed by Herbert Spencer; and (4) W. I. Thomas thought in terms of a broad social division of labor, in which the intellectuals do what the wealthy donors—public or private—want. I note in passing that Veblen and Thomas were both eminent members of the University's faculty and both were pushed out because of behavior in their private lives that was regarded as improper. Laski was an influential visitor to the University.

Theodore W. Schultz's paper, "Distortions of Economic Research," in a sense continues Laski's theme. (That may be ironic, since Schultz and Laski in their economic views are far apart.) Schultz gives an analysis of distorting pressures on academic research in economics, pressures that come from sources of funding. First, there is pressure to do immediate mission-oriented work. Second, there is pressure to come to conclusions desired by the grantor. These two kinds of forces, stemming from the seductive availability of funds, draw academic economists away from their more important missions of basic research and of fundamental social criticism. It is useful to compare the statements by Schultz and by Coleman. Both emphasize the importance of high quality in research, but Schultz sees a gulf between objective basic research and donor-nudged research on specific problems. Coleman, as I read him, sees no sharp distinction and argues for the possibility of objective research on policy-related issues . . . the more objective as the research is carried out in university-like settings.

In counterpoint to the papers by Professors Coleman, Schultz, and Karl appears a brief statement by Richard C. Atkinson, then Director of the National Science Foundation and now Chancellor of the University of California at San Diego. Atkinson describes current and recent past levels of federal research support in the social sciences. His major point is that in the social sciences—but *not* in the natural sciences—the fraction of federal research support going to universities is decreasing while that going to independent research organizations, industry, and government laboratories is in :reasing. Although Coleman and Schultz might interpret that in terms of kind and quality of research, Atkinson is careful not to draw such normative conclusions. I suppose that he is thus careful, not only because of his official NSF position when he wrote the statement, but also because he knows better than many of us about difficulties in the categories and measurement systems that led to his numbers. For example, the distinctions among basic research, applied research, and development are not only fuzzy, but fuzzy in different ways at different times. Thus there is a link between the statement by Richard Atkinson and the one by Norman M. Bradburn, next to be described.

Professor Bradburn's essay, "Discrepancies Between Concepts and Their Measurements: The Urban-Rural Example," reaches a fundamental problem related to the separate skepticisms of Cronbach and Sahlins, yet not specifically delineated by either. Bradburn draws our attention to the difficulties throughout the social sciences of going from a category or concept that seems intuitively clear to numerical measurements that are inevitably arbitrary and ambiguous. How, for example, to translate the general ideas of employment and unemployment into questions, coding, and classifications of a survey? Consider the many arbitrary decisions that go into such economic measures as gross national product or productivity indexes. Those are relatively easy questions compared with others stemming from some sociological or psychological variables. Bradburn chooses as paradigm the polar concepts urban versus rural. He shows how these ideas have been defined and measured in practice, and he points out difficulties in the operations.

Philip Converse's paper, "The Impact of the Polls on National Leadership," deals with the effects of opinion polls on major public decisions. How much effect do the polls have, and when and why? How much effect should they have? These questions relate, on the one hand, to philosophical issues about democratic governance; on the other hand, the questions lead to concrete problems of opinion poll quality, of question formation, interviewer training, and the like. Insofar as social science research leads to social science teaching, that teaching will affect public policy in part through the opinions of the educated public; we see this, I believe, in broad changes of public opinion about racial discrimination, poverty, and medical care. Converse stresses the need for careful framing and interpretation of opinion polls; a central problem for him is the degree to which misinformed, or uninformed, opinion is reported and analyzed.

The papers have further interrelationships unexplored in this brief introduction. For example, the Schultz and Sahlins essays are alike in their stress on pure research, but totally different in style and intellectual posture. Again, the measurement devices used by Peterson—for example, measuring verbal ability by a brief vocabulary test during a structured interview—might fruitfully be analyzed in the Bradburn manner. Without further ado, here are the papers themselves.

1 Are Social Problems Problems That Social Science Can Solve?

Herbert A. Simon

CARNEGIE-MELLON UNIVERSITY

The building whose ripe maturity we celebrate this week was a very young building when I entered it for the first time—in fact, it was then scarcely four years old. Although I came a little too late for the opening ceremonies that dedicated it in words of hope and promise, I have read the published report of those ceremonies and am aware of what was expected of the building and of those who would inhabit it.

Whether our gathering this week should be regarded as a rite of celebration or a judicial proceeding is an open question. Many of the titles of the talks listed in the program—including this one— read as if we intended to undertake an exercise in evaluation, perhaps to provide a report to the benefactors who paid for these stones and to assure them, if we can, that their money was well spent.

But a building, even a building as sturdy as this one, should not bear the whole weight of sustaining the social sciences and their progress. I think the record will show that it has done more than its share. Now let us turn our attention away from the building and toward the social sciences themselves. In particular, it appears to be my special task to discuss whether the social sciences can discharge the responsibility, so often assigned to them, of contributing to the solution of what we call "social problems." Are social problems problems that social science can solve?

It is often appropriate to begin an exercise like this with a few definitions. It seems especially appropriate to explicate a title that contains such contentious terms as "social problems," "social science," and "solve." Since good definitions of these terms aren't easily come by, I turned to the *International Encyclopedia of the Social Sciences* for wisdom. There, in the article on Social

I want to thank Harold Guetzkow for valuable comments on an earlier version of this paper.

1

Problems, I found (*IESS* 14:452), "Social problems are perplexing questions about human society proposed for solution." That didn't seem to help much.

However, I did find instructive and helpful the article, written by Edwin M. Lemert, that followed the definition, and I commend it to all of you. I found even more helpful, in the index volume of the encyclopedia (*IESS* 17:102), the whole list of social problems that were deemed worthy of treatment in separate articles. There are about thirty-three of them, ranging, in alphabetical order, from "aging" to "war." I will not reproduce the entire list, most elements of which will occur to you. In *Revelations* you will find a shorter, but more vivid, list: war, famine, pestilence. I will have occasion to refer to these again, using them to help us decide what is a "social problem" and what is a "solution."

What Are Social Problems Like?

Simply calling certain issues "social problems" does not place a greater responsibility on the social sciences than upon any other sciences to provide the wisdom for their solution. Proposed remedies for social problems involve changing Man's environment and improving his tools (technological fixes), changing society and inventing new social institutions (social fixes), and changing individual human beings (psychological fixes). Insofar as there is any division of labor among the sciences in these matters, the social and behavioral sciences are usually thought to be primarily responsible for providing social and psychological fixes, the natural sciences for providing technological fixes. Of course, a given problem might be attacked with combined weapons and collaborating forces; and there is no law that limits proposals to the corresponding professionals. Moreover, the game may be played by amateurs too—and frequently is.

Finding the right direction in which to look for solutions to social problems is an old conundrum. In the volume reporting the dedicatory ceremonies for this building (*The New Social Science*, 1930, pp. 36–37), one of the speakers, John C. Merriam, president of the Carnegie Institution and brother of Charles Merriam, told the following story: "I remember standing near a prison in Yucatan. The governor had just addressed the prisoners. As we stood talking over the situation, he said to me, 'Dr. Merriam, the question is, Shall we punish, educate, or operate?'"

The governor could have added several other alternatives, for example, Shall we redistribute wealth? Shall we improve burglar alarms?

Twenty-five years after Dr. Merriam's remarks, at the half-way celebration for this same building, Frank Knight addressed similar questions, concluding, with his characteristic skepticism (*The State of the Social Sciences*, p. 16): "Thus what man, the romantic, wants from social science he certainly will not get, not in a society with any freedom whatever. Prediction and control cannot be mutual; but what each naturally wants is to predict and control the rest, and wants social science to tell him how."

But the social sciences are empirical sciences. Before we succumb to either optimism or pessimism, we must look at evidence. Let's see what evidence about the nature of social problems and the routes to their solution can be provided by the examples of the three Big Problems mentioned in *Revelations*: war, famine, and pestilence. It will probably be best for us to refer to them by the broader and less flamboyant labels of war, poverty, and disease. Each of the three will illustrate for us one or more of the fundamental issues that both underlie the difficulties of solving most social problems and challenge the very meaning of terms like "solve" and "fix."

War   War is generally (though not universally or unequivocally) regarded as a state to be avoided. Some would avoid it at any cost; others would accept it, reluctantly, if the costs of the alternatives were too high. Almost no one thinks the probability of its occurring—even in the form of nuclear war—is very low.

The problem of war has not been neglected by social scientists, including a number, like Quincy Wright and Hans Morgenthau, who have practiced their profession in this building. As a result of social science inquiry, we know a great deal more about the conditions under which war occurs than we did a generation or two ago. One important conceptual advance that has occurred during the lifetime of the building has been to characterize war-breeding situations as Prisoners' Dilemma games, in which conflict of interest combined with uncertainty in mutual expectations form an unstable, lethal mixture. In a Prisoners' Dilemma game, each player chooses between a cooperative and a preemptive strategy. If both select the cooperative strategy, both fare well. If one selects the cooperative and one the preemptive strategy, the aggressor is generously rewarded and the cooperator badly punished. If both select the preemptive strategy, both are destroyed. Uncertainty and lack of trust produce instability and the potential for disaster.

In recent years, ethologists and sociobiologists have revived an old and very different conceptualization: war as an expression of deep-lying and biologically determined human aggressive traits.[1] Both of these conceptions (to the extent that they are veridical) cast light on the nature of the phenomena with which we are concerned without providing any clear prescriptions for eliminating war or making it less deadly.

If we look in the other direction, at social inventions directed toward solving the problem of war, we find that social science has made few inputs to them (and whether even these inputs are in fact substantial contributions to the solution is an entirely separate question). The contributions that have been acknowledged by the award of the Nobel Peace Prize have been very little influenced by the social sciences, with the possible exceptions of the award to Jane Addams in 1931 and to Norman Angell in 1934. Three natural scientists have received the award, two (Pauling and Sakharov) for their activities in relation to nuclear disarmament, the third (Borlaug) for his contribution to another, but possibly related, social problem: poverty. Most of the prizes have been awarded for mediating one or another belligerent situation, or for proposals or steps toward some form of organized international cooperation. Some of the prizes—for example, the one to Mother Theresa—give symbolic recognition to compassionate behavior which itself symbolizes Man's mutual sympathy for his fellowmen and his struggle to translate that sympathy into peaceful activity.

The proposals of both natural scientists and of game theorists among social scientists for reducing the probabilities of war have generally taken the form of technological fixes (e.g., deterrence) for the nuclear arms race. I do not have to explain to this audience why the social science record in this domain has been so bleak, at

1. The evolutionary argument that aggression has survival value and that aggressive traits will therefore be selected has not gone unchallenged. Donald Campbell, among others, has pointed out that in a social animal altruism may have survival value, and hence that altruistic traits may be selected. Hence the evidence for a biological basis for war seems to me inconclusive, at best.

least with respect to prescription if not to diagnosis. If the theory of games has taught us nothing else, it has taught us how difficult is the prediction of human behavior in situations involving conflict of interest combined with mutual uncertainty of intentions. In these kinds of situations (which include also the important areas of imperfect competition and political and economic bargaining), the very definition of rational choice is in question. And since the principle of rationality is our most powerful tool for predicting human behavior, we are left bare-handed when we are uncertain what rationality prescribes. If we do not know what it means to be rational, how can we say what the rational man will do? And how can we decide how we should interact with him?

Considerable ingenuity has been expended in searching for empirically verified models of human rationality under uncertainty, one of the most fruitful directions of search being the simulation of arms races and of diplomatic negotiation and bargaining. For these are the models we must have if the social sciences are to have something important to say about the whole range of situations in which human decisions rest on conjectures about the decisions of others, including those most terrible situations we call war.

If we accept the alternative, "aggressive instincts," explanation for the phenomenon of war, prescription is equally difficult, hinging on our ability to change the fundamental nature of Man. But since I regard this explanation as less plausible than the game theoretical one, I will not pursue it farther here.

Poverty   In the domain of poverty, in contrast to war, a method of solution exists and has been applied with a considerable measure of success to significant parts of the world. But, as my earlier mention of Norman Borlaug suggests, the remedy does not derive from social science knowledge. It is a technological fix: to abolish poverty, increase productivity; to increase productivity, develop and apply modern agricultural and industrial technology.

There is a good deal to be said for this prescription, which suggests that we should turn to natural science and engineering for the solution of this social problem rather than to the social sciences. That, of course, is one very common interpretation of the Industrial Revolution: that the coming of machinery and its attendant natural science created, for the first time in human history, the prospect of a world from which both poverty and human

have given us some understanding—although still not enough—of some of the factors influencing the growth of population. And perhaps most important of all, they have made us see what an elastic measuring rod we use when we measure our progress toward eliminating poverty. This last point needs some elaboration. It was Harlan Cleaveland, I think, who coined the phrase, "the revolution of rising expectations." That phrase captures two of the fundamental truths about social goals—not only poverty but others as well. First, we measure our progress toward those goals with a shrinking and expanding measuring stick. As George Stigler illustrated many years ago with his calculation of a minimum-cost adequate diet, poverty is a mental state, not a physical or physiological one. Neither he nor I mean by this that people cannot starve to death. What we mean is that removal of the danger of starvation—a goal which has not yet been achieved on a worldwide scale and which will perhaps again be jeopardy in the future—does not solve the problem of poverty, which continues to exist as long as people can imagine themselves better off than they now are and as long as they can observe others who are better off than they.

As social scientists, we know a great deal about the workings of aspiration levels, at least in modern societies, and in those that have been exposed to the modern world. A description of the human condition in terms of aspiration levels is fundamentally different from a description in terms of the standard concepts of utility. In the scale of aspirations, unlike the scale of utility, there is a natural zero point, usually located a little above the current level of living, whatever that may be. Above that zero point lies the region of satisfaction; below it, the region of dissatisfaction. If the actual standard of living moves, the zero point of the aspiration scale moves with it—in either direction, although more smoothly and rapidly upward than downward. Both intense dissatisfaction and great satisfaction are transient states that shift toward an equilibrium of mild discontent with the way things are and, usually, an urge to improve them.

The points of comparison that establish the zero of the aspiration scale are the recent past and the visible neighbor. In particular, the discovery that others have things we don't have, or have more of the things we have, exerts a potent upward pressure on aspirations. On a worldwide scale this redefines economic development as a zero-sum game. One wins this game only if one's well-being increases more rapidly than one's neighbor's. Progress is to be measured not by whether per capita food consumption or GNP increases but whether it increases more rapidly than in other countries of the world. In the worst form of the game, comparisons are made of absolute rates of increase instead of relative rates—comparisons that practically insure that the game will be won by the most highly developed nations and lost by those at a low level of development.

However the scoring is done, by defining economic progress as a zero-sum game we guarantee that the problem of poverty will have no solution—neither a social solution nor a technological fix. The problem of poverty is an excellent example, but by no means a unique one, of the way in which aspiration-level mechanisms redefine social issues so as to make them unsolvable. Proverbial wisdom carries an awareness of this dilemma—consult the entries under "ambition" in your Bartlett's *Quotations*—but game theory has given us a clearer formulation of the difficulty, and research on aspiration levels firm empirical support for it.

Disease   The third member of our triad, disease, represents a technological problem transformed into a social issue. Formerly, when ill, we sent for the doctor; now, we request health care delivery. (Anyone who can hear that latter phrase without wincing has no ear for the English language.) The change in terminology reflects a change in our view of where the problem lies. The traditional health system can be fairly described as a (biological) technological fix, operating generally through the same market mechanisms as those that provided food and the other necessities of life. As the technology became more powerful—especially with respect to contagious diseases—it acquired a public health component, also largely conceived as a biological technology.

It must have come as something of a surprise to his medical colleagues when, at the dedication ceremonies for this building in 1929, a distinguished medical school dean (Milton Winternitz of Yale) described medicine as a social science. One can interpret that claim in a number of ways. First, it constitutes a recognition that technologies (not only medicine but the others as well) do need a social "delivery system"—that they are embedded in an institutional environment. Second, it hints that the goals of medical treatment may not be definable purely in biological terms but have an essential social and psychological component as well. Third, it suggests that technical remedies for medical problems, like technical remedies for other problems, may have unsuspected indirect consequences of great significance.

The most obvious, and perhaps most studied, "systems" effect of health care is its impact on population growth. I do not think one exhibits a lack of human feeling by expressing regret that the revolutions in food-producing technology and medical technology preceded in time a revolution in the biological and social technology for controlling the sizes of populations. Both technical fixes could be of the utmost value to mankind, but will not be until we have learned how to stabilize the world's population. Of course I assume that achieving the stabilization of population by liberal application of the old remedies of war, famine, and pestilence would not be regarded as an acceptable solution.

In any event, as we range over the Big Problems, there is probably no point where social science knowledge could make a more strategic contribution than in showing the path to effective control of population size. By putting this last sentence in the future conditional, I would seem to imply that up to the present the contribution of the social sciences has not been impressive. In this matter, as in many others that I shall refer to in my talk, I am no expert. But it is probably fair to say, first, that our knowledge, as social scientists, of demographic forces and the feasible and unfeasible ways of modifying demographic trends is considerably deeper than it was when this building was dedicated; but that, second, such progress as has been made in various parts of the world toward curbing explosive population growth has mostly occurred independently of planned interventions guided by social science knowledge. So here we have had some progress, but we know enough about it so that we should probably not take the credit for it.

Another thing we have learned about progress in the health field is that it creates a whole host of social issues related to aging and dying. Not the least among these is the issue of redefining our individual and social goals as we get more and more control over the time and manner of death. The further conundrums of this kind that will have to be dealt with when cloning and the application of recombinant DNA techniques to humans become possible are only barely imaginable at the present time. We have tended to regard it as self-evident that any increase in our power to manage and control the human condition was necessarily a contribution to welfare. We have learned that increases in our power to control bring in their wake increases in our responsibility to decide. They force us to choose in situations where traditional values and modes of calculation afford us no guidance.

A case can be made for both impotence and chance as preferred modes of choice in some social situations. Nothing we know of ourselves as a species or as individuals suggests that we will be happier when we can choose or even predict the day of our death. And the responsibility for making such a choice for another human being is regarded as an almost unconscionable moral burden. Thus, in wartime, we use a lottery as part of the process of deciding which specific individuals will be exposed to the risks of battlefield death. In less solemn matters, at Las Vegas and in state lotteries, individuals happily subject themselves to the laws of chance, even though the objectively calculated expected return is negative. And, of course, we all begin life with the supreme lottery of the distribution of DNA.

Summary   What general conclusions about the application of the social sciences to societal problems can we draw from these three examples of war, poverty, and disease? From the problem of war we have learned that situations involving conflict of interest combined with uncertainty about mutual intentions are particularly intractible. The proverb says that a problem well formulated is a problem half solved. But the problem of war is a decisive counterexample to the proverb. The social sciences have shown great ingenuity and sophistication, particularly with the help of game theory and simulation techniques, in formulating the problem of war. That formulation, which I see no reason to question, makes the problem seem harder, not easier, to solve.

From the problem of poverty, we have learned that technology can indeed make a difference in the human condition; that it has, in fact, the potential for creating a world in which all will be able to meet at least their basic physiological needs. We have learned also that technology can create this result only in a suitable institutional environment; and our ignorance is still vast as to what the essential elements of such an environment are, and how it is to be brought into being. We have learned that beyond the manifest problem of poverty there lurks a latent problem of unanchored aspiration levels, and the consequent tendency of all attempts at social progress to turn into zero-sum games of envious comparison. (We could have learned that lesson much earlier by careful attention to the story of the Garden in *Genesis*.) Elimination of poverty seems as remote as the elimination of war. Both would require basic changes in the nature of Man.

From the problem of disease we have received ample confirmation of the lessons learned from the other two problems. We have learned also that when we convert an issue from one of individual behavior to one of social policy, goals that seem unproblematic at the individual level become highly ambiguous at the social level. In the domain of health, this is true both of the effects of improvement of health care upon the growth of population, and the assumption that prolongation of life is a self-evident goal that needs no examination. Moreover, we have learned that randomness, the inability to calculate precise causes and consequences, is not necessarily an unwanted element in human society.

If the social sciences have fallen short of our aspirations for them; if they have not provided simple remedies for the "big problems" of war, poverty, and disease, at the very least they have helped us to characterize these problems and to identify their major systems effects. They have encouraged us, also, to acquire attitudes of appropriate caution and tentativeness toward proposed local "fixes," whether those fixes be based on natural science or social science knowledge.

Working on the Smaller Problems

Many of the conditions we label "social problems" are less awesome than the three we have been discussing. Perhaps the social sciences, like individual human beings, will succeed better in achieving their goals if they moderate their aspirations to reasonable levels.

One way of lowering aspirations is to tackle only those issues that are commensurate in scale with the tools available for grappling with them.

Social science knowledge may be sufficiently far developed to enable us to approach some of the problems of the aged, of the educational process, of decision making in organizations, or of crime that are often regarded as being within the domain of professional social science practice.

Models of Professional Activity   The characteristic point of view of the professional man—whether engineer, physician, or architect—is not that he is responsible for dealing with the problems *of* society, but only for dealing with problems *in* society. Once he abandons the "big problems" for more manageable ones, the applied social scientist can adopt a similar posture and can regard his role as a professional one, closely comparable with roles of the traditional professions.

Anyone who takes a professional stance must think clearly about three questions:

1. Who is the client? Whose goals is the professional seeking to implement?

2. Is society the patient, or are individuals? Who and what is to be changed?

3. What are the strategic variables that are to be regarded as controllable? What is taken as fixed and what as changeable?

In short, the professional needs to know with whom he works and with what powers. The answers to these questions depend on the model we adopt of the solution process. At least three distinct models of professional activity immediately suggest themselves: the engineering or medical model, the legislative reference model, and the public diffusion model. Let me explain what I mean by each of these.

In engineering and medicine, the professional man is engaged by and serves a client in the furtherance of the client's goals. He designs a machine or a structure that the client wants built, or he undertakes to cure an ailment from which the client is suffering. Whether the machine will serve a useful social purpose or whether the client's life is worth saving is not usually thought to be one of the professional's concerns. He is a "gun for hire"— always within the limits of the law, of professional expertise, and of the ethical norms of the profession.

The legislative reference model is my label for situations in which the professional person provides advice or expert knowledge to a legislative body or other public agency. This model differs from the engineering or medical model primarily in the nature of the client. From that difference, however, follow others. The goals and values to be served are now social ones, instead of goals and values of a private individual. As a consequence, the goals may be vaguer and less operational than in the private professional-client relation. Moreover, the legislature as client is likely to be in a less dependent relation with the professional than is the private individual as client.

The public diffusion model describes that wide class of situations where the social scientist incorporates his knowledge or advice in a book or article (or in a speech) and diffuses it through the various channels of publication (or communication). Knowledge diffused in these ways may consist of specific advice on very specific issues, or it may be fundamental knowledge about the human condition. What distinguishes this model is that the advice or knowledge is directed to a broad audience—in the limit, to the whole public. Again, I will consider some examples that illuminate the differences among these various models of professional activity and the significance of those differences.

Compensatory Education   A number of important social science inputs—from sociology and educational psychology—were made into the "Sesame Street" program, and these inputs can undoubtedly claim an important share of credit for the quality of the program. What is the appropriate model of professional activity within which to view those contributions? If we take the viewpoint of the legislative reference model, then a major goal of "Sesame Street" was to equalize educational opportunity among the different socioeconomic classes; to give underprivileged children a better chance to compete with those whose home environments offered them greater advantages.

On the other hand, if we apply the engineering model to "Sesame Street," we will probably view the goal as one of producing television shows that will educate children—provide them with certain basic knowledge about letters and words. By this standard, if the programs are watched by many children, and if the children learn from them, they are a success.

It is clear that such an activity could be viewed as highly successful in terms of the engineering model but a failure in terms of the legislative reference model. If children learn a great deal from the programs, but the advantaged learn more than the disadvantaged, then it meets the narrower objectives but not the broader social ones. We are then put in the position of having to weigh the systems effects of the activity against the concrete results that, in a typical professional-client relation, would be regarded as fully desirable.

This dilemma is by no means limited to the specific example of "Sesame Street" but arises in any attempt we might make to evaluate educational institutions or educational technology. Our evaluations are going to be quite different as we assume different models of professional activity to be appropriate.

Organizational Decision Making   The effectiveness of business and public organizations in our society depends heavily on the quality of the decisions made in them. A growing number of social science professionals are engaged in improving the decision-making processes in organizations through applying operations research techniques (e.g., linear programming or queuing theory) to scheduling or inventory decisions, or techniques of heuristic search derived from the field of cognitive science.

Within the framework of the engineering or medical models, there is no ambiguity about the goals of these activities. They are aimed at increasing human competence in organizational tasks, hence enhancing the productivity of the organizations. Viewed within a broader framework, the implicit assumption is always present that organizational effectiveness contributes to desirable social goals. From a social standpoint, activities carried on with the engineering-medical model are valuable only if the existing institutional and organizational structure is fundamentally sound. As is well known, this model of professional activity is essentially conservative in its assumptions, and inappropriate for persons who question the institutional structure in which the activity takes place. Revolutionaries gain no satisfaction from strengthening existing institutions.

Both of my examples—compensatory education and improving decision making—refer to domains where the social sciences are patently capable of producing results, at least within the engineering-medical model. The powers of operations research and modern cognitive science to bring about reliable effects is substantial and growing. What is problematic, again, about these examples are the systems effects when the situations are viewed in terms of social goals. Even when we are dealing with (apparently) bite-size problems, systems effects cannot be avoided or ignored.

The American Race Problem   Let me conclude with an example of a somewhat different sort: the task of achieving racial equality in America. Here there is little ambiguity about the goals, and the relevant professional models are the legislative reference model and the public diffusion model. School integration measures provide a good example of the role of social science knowledge within the former model.

Serious movement toward school integration in the United States is usually dated from the decision of the United States Supreme Court in *Brown* v. *Board of Education of Topeka*. The Court's opinion in the *Brown* case contained numerous citations of empirical evidence from social science sources. Most of this evidence had not been prepared specifically for the Court but was already in the public domain—a point on which I shall comment presently. In recent years, however, a number of widely known pieces of research have been carried out with the specific aim of evaluating the effects of integration, especially its effects on the motivations, emotions, and rates of learning of minority students. The unanticipated (or at least unintended) systems effects of integration, such as the movement of white families to the suburbs, have also been assessed.

While the problems of integration appear to be about as knotty as they were two decades ago, and while the social science knowledge that has been brought to bear has been less definitive in answering critical questions than one might wish, still, I think integration provides an excellent example of the application of the legislative reference model. If the social problem has not been fully solved, it is because it involves exceedingly difficult and complex issues, and probably not because of our ignorance of causes and consequences—though much ignorance remains. As with the Big Problems, no simple social or technological fix is in sight.

With respect to racial equality in general, we can be more

sanguine—here enormous progress has been made in three decades. And here, the public diffusion model is the most relevant. I refer in particular to the impact of Gunnar Myrdal's *An American Dilemma* (1942). By the very fact that its channels of impact are diffuse, it is difficult or impossible to trace in detail how a book like this one secures its effect, or even to measure the magnitude of that effect. So I am mainly repeating folk wisdom, and not citing hard evidence (unless the citations in the *Brown* case are such evidence) that *An American Dilemma* did, in fact, have great impact. (In another problem domain, Rachel Carson's *Silent Spring* presents a second example of a surely large, but unmeasured, impact.)

If *An American Dilemma* did play a significant role in melting the iceberg of racial patterns, what was the mechanism? First, the book provided a thoroughly documented description of the situation of blacks in America and of black-white relations. It held up a mirror to ourselves in a way that made it difficult to doubt the accuracy of the reflected image. Second, it analyzed the attitudes of white Americans about the situation, and their beliefs about it. It brought latent attitudes to conscious attention, in particular, contradictions between beliefs in human equality and the realities of the treatment of blacks.

The third characteristic of the Myrdal volume is that it did not conceal its own value premises but, while preserving objectivity in its analysis, communicated clearly the moral indignation of its author. *Silent Spring* had this same quality and this same combination of description and judgment. It seems likely that the tone of these books was an essential ingredient of their political effectiveness. It would be interesting to try to discover counterexamples—books that had wide public diffusion and impact but only provided analysis without taking an explicit position on values. I have been unable to think of such counterexamples.

Human Freedom   Although it seems not entirely appropriate to list it under "small problems," I cannot conclude without making further reference to a problem that only a few societies have solved, of maintaining a wide range of human freedom of thought, speech, and action. In the passage from Frank Knight that I quoted earlier, he expressed considerable pessimism about the compatibility of freedom with the use of social science knowledge to handle social issues. Is freedom incompatible with prediction and control? If the social game we are playing is a zero-sum game, the answer is probably, "yes." But if the game is not zero sum, there is no reason why freedom should imply unpredictability or why control should not be directed *primarily* toward the environment. That is the meaning, of course, of calls for "a moral equivalent of war." If we can place the locus of our problems in the environment rather than defining them as a war against each other, then we can also conceive of collaborative effort to achieve common goals.

There are surely many other facets to the problem of freedom. To mention only one, there is the dilemma posed so poignantly by *The Clockwork Orange*. Does freedom encompass the freedom to be vicious? And what is the price, in terms of encroachment on freedom and even on the core of what we call the "human" in us, of changing people in order to exorcise viciousness from them? These are partly questions of value, but they are also partly factual questions about the psychological and biological nature of our species.

Conclusion

In the light of the examples we have examined, what can we conclude about the efficacy of the social sciences in solving social problems? Where can the social sciences make their most useful contributions?

With respect to what I have called "small problems," there are opportunities for the application of social science knowledge within all the models of professional activity we have considered: the engineering-medical model, the model of legislative assistance, and the public diffusion model. Nor is it hard to find examples of domains where the social sciences have played, and are playing, a significant constructive role.

With respect to the Big Problems, the past and potential contribution of the social sciences would seem to lie mainly in gaining a deeper understanding of social institutions and processes, and—of greatest importance—a deeper understanding of ourselves. Little will be gained by trying to apply the engineering and medical models to the big problems—and this independently of whether we have social fixes or technological fixes in view.

Since social science is itself a component of our social institutions, one possible direction of progress in social science could be toward answering the question posed by the title of this paper: Are social problems problems that social science can solve? I think we have already made some progress in this direction in recent years, and as evidence of that progress I should like to read two quotations, one dating from 1942, when this building was only a dozen years old, the other from 1976. The first is from *An American Dilemma*:

> The rationalism and moralism which is the driving force behind social study, whether we admit it or not, is the faith that institutions can be improved and strengthened and that people are good enough to live a happier life. With all we know today, there should be the possibility to build a nation and a world where people's great propensities for sympathy and cooperation would not be so thwarted.... We have today in social science a greater trust in the improvability of man and society than we have ever had since the Enlightenment. [P. 1024]

The second quotation is from the report of a committee of the National Academy of Sciences entitled, *Social and Behavioral Science Programs in the National Science Foundation* (I should perhaps disclose that I was chairman of the committee):

> The too-casual application of new ideas emerging from social science research has the same potential for producing often unwanted consequences as does the premature application of natural science discoveries.... Because of this, a very large part of applied social science research is evaluation, providing knowledge about present and future effects that is relevant to the daily decisions confronting legislators and administrators.... Perhaps the most important contribution the social and behavioral sciences can make to society is to provide, through basic and applied research, the means for better understanding of the consequences and uncertainties of all kinds of change as well as the consequences of no change at all. [P. 22]

The contrast between these two quotations captures, I think, the reining in of our aspirations for social science that has taken place in the last quarter or third of a century. I don't equate the sobering with pessimism but rather with a maturing in our understanding of what social problems really are. It reflects the progress of social science knowledge itself—including knowledge of how social institutions change and how these changes affect mankind.

The history of science, itself a social science, has taught us that we cannot usually predict in what ways, good or bad, new knowledge will be applied. Before we create knowledge we have to place our bets that the balance will be on the bright side or on the dark. In placing our bets we have only the general record of human history as our guide. Our myths tell us both of the bright knowledge conferred on us by Prometheus and the dark knowledge brought by Pandora. My reading of history leads me to accept the myth of Prometheus. On balance, knowing is better than ignorance—with respect to both natural and social phenomena.

Faith in Prometheus is the gamble we take when we claim that social science does and can contribute to the solution of social problems. After what I hope is an open-eyed review of the evidence, I, for one, conclude that it is a gamble worth taking.

2 Effects of Credentials, Connections, and Competence on Income

Paul E. Peterson
UNIVERSITY OF CHICAGO

The Social Science Research Building was established fifty years ago in a confident mood. According to the preface to the papers presented in celebration of its establishment, the articles "testify abundantly to a feeling of confidence among social science researchers; confidence not so much in results achieved as in prospects" (White 1956, p. 5). Although optimism was later disturbed by events in Germany and the Soviet Union, it remained sufficiently intact during subsequent decades that as late as 1956 Leonard White, writing the introduction to the twenty-fifth anniversary volume, could assert that "the social science faculty at the University of Chicago enter the second quarter century in their tightly packed building with courage and confidence. They know that their role in the evolving society of the future is important, even as they refuse to overestimate their capacity to control ... events" (ibid., p. xi). Because we cannot echo this theme so confidently a quarter century later, it is appropriate to consider briefly the philosophical grounds upon which it stood.

The Social Science Research Building, as so much else in the social sciences, owed much to the Progressive spirit. Social scientists at the University of Chicago and elsewhere believed that society was rapidly changing, that the forces for change were diverse and mutually responsive, and that the end results would yield a happier world. They also believed that the use of a finely honed, scientifically trained intelligence could modify these processes of change so as to hasten the rapidity with which better

An earlier version of this paper was published as "Connections, Credentials, or Competence: Declining Significance of Social Class," in *Research in Public Policy Analysis and Management: Basic Theory, Methods and Perspectives*, vol. 2, ed. John P. Crecine (Greenwich, Conn.: J.A.I. Press, 1981).

21

days arrived. And they had confidence in the ultimate good judgment of the citizens of their society. The concepts they used—social group, social role, and social action—testified to the diversity and complexity of society. And it was this very complexity that gave them confidence that the possibilities for gradual, constructive change were everywhere present. Within this spirit the great Chicago "schools" in the social sciences were constructed.

Nowhere was this confident optimism more appropriately expressed than with respect to the processes of formal education. At Chicago, as elsewhere, scholars viewed the rapid growth of educational institutions as one of the finest illustrations of the power of progressive forces. With increased schooling citizens would be better able to participate in political life, and with increased schooling citizens would be free to pursue their economic destiny unfettered by class, ethnic, or religious origins. Not only did a constantly expanding educational system affirm the worthiness of their own calling but its public benefits were almost beyond question. Charles Merriam, the founder of the Chicago school of political science and a key figure in the establishment of this building, was in fact so committed to education as a critical mechanism for achieving his progressive ideals that he devoted much of his time and energy to the study of what he called "civic education" (Karl, 1974, chap. 9).

In recent decades the Progressive spirit has nearly evaporated. It is no longer conceded that the expert and the professional have access to an esoteric body of knowledge that is used for the public good. It is no longer believed that public bureaucracies can become rationalized institutions that efficiently pursue public objectives. It is no longer claimed that citizens can ever be so well informed that they can choose wisely among alternative public policies.[1] And with this decline in confidence, the élan which

---

1. Even during the Progressive era, not all observers of political life believed that citizens were well-informed members of the political community. Graham Wallas, in *Human Nature in Politics*, was among those who expressed their doubts. Yet the Progressive era is marked by its unusual optimism. Many of the more articulate writers of the period had a special confidence in at least the potential capacity of the citizens for meaningful political participation. In this regard, the writings of John Dewey were especially influential. Later writers are more pessimistic about even the "potential" for the same kind of political involvement. See, e.g., Schumpeter (1942).

once motivated the great growth in the social sciences no longer asserts itself. Many of those working in the social sciences hesitate to address the great issues about which earlier scholars could speak with conviction. And many, perhaps, no longer believe that they provide a program of instruction that has much practical use. Instead, fractionated specializations and narrow methodological problems engage the workmanlike attention of the scholarly community.

If the decline in the Progressive spirit has left an intellectual vacuum, it has been filled at least partially by two contrasting traditions. On the right, neoconservatives have questioned the performances of public institutions by holding as an analytical standard of comparison the perfectly competitive market, whose workings in practice we have yet to see. On the left, neo-Marxists have criticized the institutions of the welfare state, claiming that they are carefully modulated so as to sustain a system of class dominance. At times, the left and the right find themselves pretty much in agreement concerning the quality of public services provided. Where they disagree is in the intrepretation. What is interpreted by the right as inevitable inefficiency in the public sector is interpreted by the left as the self-conscious product of a self-perpetuating capitalist elite. When faced with comparable arguments from right and left fifty and more years ago, progressive social scientists relied on a more or less well-integrated set of doctrines to proclaim a liberal alternative. They no longer seem willing or able to do so.

If educational policy provided the outstanding example of the Progressive commitment in previous generations, it provides no less the quintessential case of the transformation that has occurred in the social sciences in recent decades. If schools were once sacrosanct, today they are said to be almost dispensable. For example, James Coleman et al's (1966) massive report on schooling in America has been interpreted by many to say that schools have little effect on the abilities of children attending them. Those on the right have drawn upon these and related findings to argue for reduced commitment to public schooling. Those on the left have developed a more complex assessment. On the one hand, neo-Marxists agree with those on the right that schooling has little if any effects on verbal abilities. On the other hand, they claim that schooling provides an efficacious mechanism for the transmission of class domination from one generation to the next. Although schools do not provide educational opportunities for children, they do provide them with a set of credentials that give young adults differential access to the marketplace. And because these credentials are handed out unevenly, the dominant social classes solidify their privileged place in American society.

The persuasive force of these new interpretations of American institutions seems to be quite independent of any empirical evidence that supports them. The inability of liberal-minded social scientists to respond effectively to critics on either the left or the right seems more a function of their own lack of self-confidence than of any new information about social relationships in American society. If anything, recent evidence with respect to educational policy suggests that the Progressive ideal is better approximated today than ever before.

The single most influential neo-Marxist analysis of educational policy written in the past decade is entitled *Schooling in Capitalist America.* Written by Samuel Bowles and Herbert Gintis (1976), this study argues that "education reproduces inequality by justifying privilege and attributing poverty to personal failure" (p. 114). Schools function to reproduce class dominance by providing differential educational opportunities to members of different social classes. Although Bowles and Gintis utilize a range of data to develop their argument, their case depends heavily on an imaginative, if seriously flawed, analysis of the relative importance of class background, education, and ability as determinants of earned income. According to their results, income is largely a function of either the direct influence of one's class background or the influence of one's years of schooling, itself highly dependent on family socioeconomic status. Any effect of ability, as measured by intelligence or verbal ability tests, is insignificant, once class background and schooling are controlled.

From these results, Bowles and Gintis draw the conclusions that the main factors that affect income are connections and credentials. Since ability has little influence on income, whatever impact schooling has on ability is of little use to the future breadwinner. On the other hand, the credentials that advanced schooling provide, supplemented by the connections that are a part of a privileged social background, provide great continuity in the patterns of social dominance across generations.

There are at least three reasons for questioning these conclusions. First, their analysis has serious technical flaws, which Karplus and I have discussed elsewhere (1979). Second, their research findings, based on surveys conducted in 1962 and 1964, are dated. Third, their interpretation of the results leaves much to be desired. Simply because education has an effect on income separate and apart from the effect of a person's general ability does not indicate that earnings received are merely a function of educational "credentials." Although general ability is one qualification an employer values, in addition he can be expected to look for more particular sets of skills that may well have been enhanced by specific educational experiences. Indeed, had education no effect on income independent of a person's general ability and family background, then it would be reasonable to conclude that the consequences of schooling were little more than distributing credentials and confirming inequality. Indeed, it is rather perverse to use information that finds a substantial relationship between education and income as a basis for making an argument that schools do little to equalize opportunities in American society.

Despite these flaws, this study of *Schooling in Capitalist America* has been used extensively in basic courses on the social foundations of education, has been frequently cited as providing useful information about schooling by those in policymaking positions, and has been an important document for many popular assessments of our educational system. Because the work has had wide circulation in both academic and popular circles, it seemed appropriate to undertake a replication of the analysis on more recently collected data. Fortunately, the National Opinion Research Center (NORC) collected relevant information from a sample of the U.S. adult population as part of its General Social Survey conducted in the years 1974, 1976, and 1978 (Davis 1978).

Susan Karplus and I are currently using this data to analyze the determinants of income. In this report of our analysis, the measure of income is the respondent's report of his earned income from his primary occupation during the preceding year. Education is the number of years of schooling the respondent reported that he had completed. The measure of family social class background reported here is an index which weights equally father's occupation, parental income, father's education, mother's education, and the number of siblings in the family. The estimate of the respondent's verbal ability is obtained from a vocabulary test originally used by Thorndike and Gallup in their study of the intelligence of the American population. Thorndike and Gallup selected this test for two reasons: (1) of all the specific tests of ability, the vocabulary test has the highest correlation with general intelligence; (2) a vocabulary test is most easily administered to a national sample of respondents by interviewers untrained in the art of psychological testing. Thorndike and Gallup estimate the reliability of their test at about .85. NORC's 50 percent sample of the Thorndike-Gallup test can be expected to have a somewhat lower coefficient of reliability.

In order to test the hypotheses advanced by Bowles and Gintis, we constructed a recursive path model as outlined in figure 1. Income is treated as a function of socioeconomic status, education, and ability. It is further assumed that education and ability are in part a function of family SES. No assumptions are made as to whether ability is causally prior to education or vice versa. The

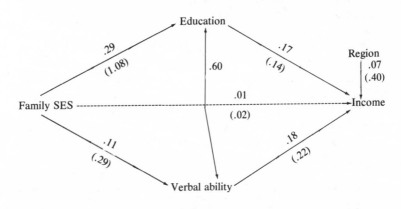

$R^2 = .11$

$N = 731$

Variance (income) = .29

Total effects

SES = .12

Ed. = .19

V.A. = .28

Fig. 1　Path analysis of the determinant of income for white males (25–64), 1976. Coefficient not in parenthesis: standardized B; coefficient in parenthesis: unstandardized B solid arrow: B more than twice standard error dotted arrow: B less than twice standard error.

region of the country in which a person worked was included as a control variable.

When information concerning white males between the ages of 25 and 64 was analyzed within the framework of this model, the results failed to confirm the Bowles-Gintis connection. First, family SES, education, and income were not closely linked in such a way that perpetuated class domination across generations. Instead, the findings revealed a pattern of very loosely connected social relationships. Moreover, the effects on income of family SES were especially weak and insignificant. Not only was there no discernible direct effect of family SES on income at all, but even when the indirect effects of family background, as mediated by education and ability, were taken into account, the total effects yielded a coefficient of only .12.

Second, the findings show that the marketplace values the general ability of individuals, regardless of their class or educational backgrounds. Indeed, measured verbal ability seems to be a substantially more important determinant of income than is the family's SES. Finally, education is also an important determinant of income, but access to educational systems is not a prerogative of the well-to-do. On the contrary, a long history of publicly supported educational institutions has left the relationship between family background and schooling severely attenuated. And the schooling one receives is valued by the marketplace much more than any "connections" one might have simply because of one's class background.

Analysis of these data by age cohort suggests some interesting changes over the last fifty years. In figure 2 white males are divided into three groups: those aged 55–64, 35–54, and 25–34. Another way of looking at these age cohorts is to understand that the oldest came of age during the depression, the middle-aged turned twenty-one during the peace and prosperity Americans enjoyed after World War II, and the youngest are the sixties or Vietnam generation. When working with data of this sort, it is difficult to distinguish the separate effects of the point in the life cycle that an individual has reached from the effects of the historical experiences of his generation. As a result, both life cycle and generational effects are very likely shaping the pattern of relationships presented in figure 2.

The most striking finding in the figure is the general loosening of

A. Ages 55–64 (Depression generation)

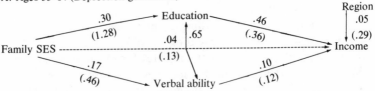

R² = .31
N = 114
Variance (income) = .32

Total effects
SES = .26
Ed. = .52
V.A. = .40

B. Ages 35–54 (postwar generation)

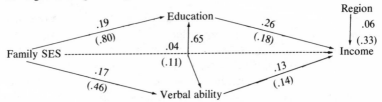

R² = .15
N = 316
Variance = .25

Total effects
SES = .16
Ed. = .34
V.A. = .30

C. Ages 25–34 (sixties generation)

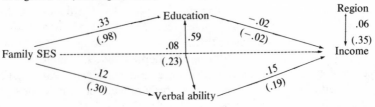

R² = .04
N = 301
Variance = .31

Total effects
SES = .12
Ed. = .07
V.A = .14

FIG. 2. Path analysis of the determinants of income for white males in 1976, by age cohort.

the American social structure across the three age cohorts. The amount of variance explained by the model declines steadily from the older to the younger white males. Also the total effects of family SES decline over time. Third, the effects of education on income decline. Only the direct effects of verbal ability maintain themselves or perhaps slightly increase.

The differences between the youngest and the middle-age group of males are probably best explained in terms of life-cycle effects. For young males, the relationship between education and income is depressed because the educated have yet to realize their full income potential. During their early adult lives, the better-educated men have less job experience than the less educated, and only when this deficiency in experience is overcome do the educated males demonstrate their full earning potential. When we controlled for these differences in experience, the importance of education for the income of the young men was not significantly different from its importance for the middle-aged group.

The difference between the oldest and the middle-aged males, on the other hand, are probably best explained as generational differences. Before World War II educational opportunities were more limited, and family background probably played a larger role in shaping the child's future. When the demand for educated labor rapidly increased after the war, the few who had received advanced training were able to realize substantial dividends on their investments in education. After World War II the educational system expanded rapidly, veterans were given an unusual opportunity to receive additional training at low cost to themselves, and the supply of educated labor increased relative to the market demand. One result seems to be a decrease in the returns on educational investment. Another seems to be a decrease in the rigidity of the social structure. In the postwar period, it seems, the family's social class background has had a declining effect on earned income.

Our analysis of the determinants of the income of white women is still in progress, but preliminary analysis does not reveal major differences in the role of family background. For blacks, the results, as reported in figure 3, are quite different. For this racial minority, the pattern of relationships was so different from the patterns identified among white males that we are reporting the results even though they are based on a wholly inadequate sample size. Further research is essential before any firm conclusions can be reached, but it is of interest to note that, among the small number of black males in our sample, family SES had a significant effect on earned income. At the same time, verbal ability was of trivial importance. Indeed, were it not for the fact that the sample size is small, the claim that income differences among blacks are a function of connections and credentials, not of competence, would almost seem warranted.

Perhaps because of long-entrenched racial practices, the marketplace may be unable to distinguish the competencies of blacks apart from their family background or the credentials they have obtained. Scholars such as Bowles and Gintis, who have emphasized the continuing importance of social class in white America, may have constructed an argument that is applicable instead for black Americans. Only recently has American public policy seriously attempted to eliminate patterns of racial prejudice and discrimination, and it is premature to evaluate the success of these government programs. Apart from their continued enforcement over long periods of time, they cannot eliminate for blacks the impact of class background on income. But it is not too soon to note that the emphasis on changing the opportunity in black America remains an area of critical concern.

Except for black Americans, the influence of social class on opportunity has declined. The evidence presented thus far has been limited to comparisons among age cohorts. But in table 1 we present another set of data which points in the same direction. This table presents the simple correlations between a number of family background characteristics and the income of American males. In addition to the NORC data, we report findings from the Occupational Changes in a Generation survey presented in the recent publication by Christopher Jencks and associates (1979). Since the data reported by Jencks et al. are collected by somewhat different techniques, comparisons across surveys must be made cautiously. But when the annual surveys conducted by NORC are compared to one another, they reveal the same declining significance of social class for males during the last half of the 1970s that Jencks et al. reported for the preceding decade. If these results are supported by further studies, one could reasonably conclude that the importance of connections as a de-

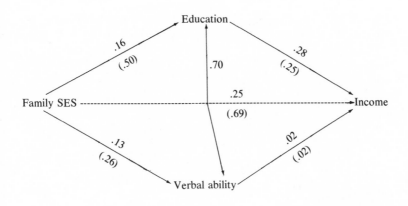

	Total effects
R² = .21	SES = .31
N = 46	Ed. = .29
Variance (income) = .34	V.A. = .22

Fɪɢ. 3   Path analysis of the determinants of income for black males (25–64), 1976.

terminant of income, however important in the past generations, is coming to an end—at least for white males.

If these changes are continuing down to 1980, it implies a certain limitation on the social sciences as tools for policy analysis. It takes a long time for research problems to be identified, quality data to be selected, analysis to be undertaken, publication to occur, and, finally, circulation of the ideas generated by the research into the public and policymaking arenas. Indeed, the time period is so protracted that by the time the findings are widely disseminated and accepted they may no longer be correct. Bowles and Gintis depended almost exclusively on data collected in the early sixties. In many of the more popular statements of the results of their research, the findings are treated as information about the current state of society. For example, in a special *New York Times* feature, Richard deLone, the author of the popular book *Small Futures,* asserts confidently that "although being poor does not guarantee that one will remain poor, it makes it far more likely" (Bennetts 1979, p. A14). Our data show that parental income and son's income was correlated in 1977–78 at the .06

TABLE 1   Simple Relationship between Family Background Characteristics and Income of All Males, in 1962, 1973, 1974, 1975–76, and 1977–78.

Background Characteristics	Correlation with Income				
	1962 (OCG)	1973 (OCG)	1974 (NORC)	1975–76 (NORC)	1977–78 (NORC)
Father's education	.220	.182	.153	.136	.030
Father's occupation	.301	.228	.196	.095	.057
Mother's education		.180	.125	.061	−.016
Parental income		.231	.049	.118	.061
Fewer siblings	.184	.162	.145	.145	.104
Non-south (childhood)	.195	.118	.029	.175	.131
Non-rural (childhood)	.166	.146	.121	.123	.115
Father's presence in family	.063	.032	.068	.045	.012
Index (all items weighed equally)			.205	.201	.119

level, a statistic seldom dignified with the phrase "far more likely."

These canards are now treated as sage observations of contemporary society. They are handy shells in the armory used by those generals and lieutenants who feel compelled to search and destroy the Great Society and its social reform policies. Some might say that inasmuch as these radical prophets provide social-scientific weaponry for those who wish to dismantle recent policy innovations, they may someday produce the very consequences they presently decry. But in our view, that places too little weight on the fundamental openness and responsiveness of American institutions.

This occasion calls for one more concluding comment. If one can generalize from the arena of educational policy to public policy as a whole, then the evidence seems to suggest that the recent incapacity of the social sciences to defend public institutions from their critics on the left is not because defense is impossible. These critics have achieved their popularity not because of the validity of their analysis but because their findings are presented with ardor and conviction in an intellectual context where these virtues are now seldom displayed. When the social scientific community regains a sense of its own capacities, when it regains the vigor which animated the founders of Eleven Twenty-six, then the contributions to public policy by the social sciences will once again be shaped both by a recognition of the progress that has been achieved and the need for continuing change and reform.

REFERENCES

Bennetts, Leslie. "Carnegie Finds Status, Not Brains, Makes a Child's Future." *New York Times* (August 24, 1979).
Bowles, Samuel, and Gintis, Herbert. *Schooling in Capitalist America*. New York: Basic Books, 1976.
Coleman, James S., et al. *Equality of Educational Opportunity*. Washington, D. C.: Government Printing Office, 1966.
Davis, James W. "General Social Surveys, 1972–78: Cumulative Codebook." Mimeographed. Chicago: National Opinion Research Center, University of Chicago, 1978.
Jencks, Christopher, et al. *Who Gets Ahead? The Determinants of Economic Success in America*. New York: Basic Books, 1979.
Karl, Barry D. *Charles E. Merriam and the Study of Politics*. Chicago: University of Chicago Press, 1974.
Peterson, Paul E., and Karplus, Susan Sherman. "Horatio Alger Is Not Dead, Despite What Bowles and Gintis Say." Paper prepared for presentation before the Research Conference on Public Policy and Management, October 1979, Chicago. Mimeographed.
Schumpeter, Joseph A. *Capitalism, Socialism and Democracy*. New York: Harper & Bros., 1942.
Wallas, Graham. *Human Nature in Politics*. New York: Alfred A. Knopf, Inc., 1921.
White, Leonard Dupee. *The State of the Social Sciences*. Papers presented at the 25th Anniversary of the Social Science Research Building. Chicago: University of Chicago Press, 1956.

3 Individual Experience and Cultural Order

Marshall Sahlins

UNIVERSITY OF CHICAGO

I am going to resurrect an issue that anthropologists these days hate to think about, even though as students of culture they have a main responsibility for discussing it. I mean the problem of "cultural determinism," or the relation between individual action and cultural order. True that an older generation with some strong ideas on the subject has now died off and a younger one having other preoccupations taken its place; and, while such is the normal definition of progress in the social sciences, we are not really free to forget the problems that plagued the ancestors. The issue was important, and besides we have been speaking it all this time while pretending not to know it. What I propose to do is reflect (in a much too schematic way) on the implications of current interests in symbolism and structuralism for the received idea that culture is sui generis, a so-called superorganic object independent of the human subjects who enact it.

Utilitarian Individualism and Cultural Determinism

It has to be recalled that the concept of the superorganic developed in anthropology—and also, with the Durkheimian "social fact," in sociology—by opposition to the complete theory of culture already present in Western society and consciousness—present, indeed, as the way this society takes consciousness of itself. I refer to the mainstream idea of an "economic man" whose rational choices precipitate, as if by an Invisible Hand, not only the well-being of the Nation but its very social forms. Marxism perhaps excepted, this utilitarian individualism is the only coherent analysis of culture the West has produced. Our colleagues in the University of Chicago Economics Department are brilliantly engaged in quantitative demonstrations of it, but even on the basis of naive experience we can be sure in advance of

35

their success. For since the development of the self-regulating market we have had this certain, if peculiar, knowledge of ourselves as businesslike social beings, bent on maximizing life's benefits and minimizing its costs. Utility dominates the study of culture," as A. M. Hocart said, "because it dominates the culture that studies."

Rendering all kinds of goods and services commensurable in their capacity as monetary values, the market society did not merely disguise to itself the meaningful differences between things. To an anthropologist, the historical peculiarity is that the kinds of acts he recognizes in a tribal context as instances of "social organization," politics," "kinship," "art," even "religion," appear, when he returns from the field, as so many quests for "utilities." For in the context of a total market, no matter what the nature of such acts taken in themselves, our relationship to them is decisively economic. Whether one chooses to go to a baseball game or a concert, provide a decent education for the children, or perhaps visit the grandparents in Florida over Christmas, all such actions and options must first be translated into their apparent common denominator of "pleasures" or "satisfactions," among which we prudently allocate our limited pecuniary means. In the translation, then, their distinctive social content is lost, with the result that from the natives' point of view all of culture seems constituted by (and as) the businesslike economizing of autonomous individuals. I have to admit that many Western anthropologists have been tempted to reproduce this indigenous folklore in their own studies, as a consciousness also of the others. For when a society makes a fetish of the commodity, its anthropology is disposed to make a commodity out of the fetish.

Bourgeois life turns culture into the hidden a priori of a calculus of pragmatic action. The symbolic order is subsumed in hierarchies of means and ends, as motives and interests located within the subject and realized by a process of rational choice also natural to him/her. Culture thus become a presupposition, we are left unaware of other logics inscribed in our intentions. I refer not merely to the difficulties of making other judgments of a Weberian sort on rational action; for example, that the collective disutilities of a system of private transport are not envisioned in the way that buying and driving a car, as a project of economizing, appears in personal experience. More significant yet is the qualitatively different logic of symbolic value that enters into action as an unreflected premise. For instance, what is the ground of our preference for outer "meats" of food animals rather than the "innards," whose déclassé status is distinctly signified by names the same as human organs ("heart," "kidneys," "lungs")? Or why do we tabu as food certain nutritious creatures, such as dogs and horses, whom we instead take into human society in the capacity of subjects, bestowing on them proper names and the status of interlocutors in human conversation? In fact, we act economically on a sustained set of anticannibalistic metaphors that have nothing to do with practical values—*except to determine them*. Or again, steak is a masculine food, thus most appropriate to the training table of the Chicago Bears, in opposition to the femininity of salads (especially tomatoes). But since all such distinctions are merely unstated premises of actions we know as the maximization of "utility," even as we can see that social arrangements are sedimented by them, mainstream social science hastens to make its own the Benthemite principle that "society is a fictitious body, the sum of the individual members who compose it." Society is no more than the contracts rational men and women enter into in the pursuit of their several private interests.

Yet as Nietzsche remarked, "Man does not seek happiness; only Englishmen do that." Anthropology has been forced to reconcile its own cultural presuppositions with the experience of other natives. In the event, the indigenous Western concepts were turned inside out. The response to individualism was to alienate man from his own activity and creativity, transferring these instead to a kind of supersubject, Culture, to whom were accorded all powers of movement and determination. Admittedly this "culture" had no phenomenal existence apart from human beings, but it had autonomous characteristics and functions, and men could do no more than express its internal constitution and dynamics. The naive consciousness of capitalist society was thus exchanged for its historic Unhappy Consciousness.

A. L. Kroeber and L. A. White (Ph.D., Chicago, 1925) were the main American prophets of the Superorganic Being. Saddled, however, with a new series of contradictions—a nonsubstantial yet active being, a collectivity with the characteristics of an individual organism, and a mind subsisting independently of human subjects—anthropologists were forced to invent highly metaphorical descriptions of this "culture," and of its relationships to people. For White, the individual finally became a particle in the magnetic field of his culture, or else a pilotless airplane controlled by radio waves:

> The human organism lives and moves within an ethical magnetic field, so to speak. Certain social forces, culturally defined, impinge on the organism and move it this way and that, toward the good, away from the bad. The organism experiences these forces though he may mistake their source. He calls this experience conscience. His behavior is analogous to a pilotless aircraft controlled by radio. The plane is directed this way and that by impulses external to it. These impulses are received by a mechanism and are then transmitted to motors, rudders, etc. This receiving and behavior-controlling mechanism is analogous to conscience.

To sum up: utilitarianism concealed culture within a faulty human epistemology, while the "superorganic" dissolved humanity in a fantastic cultural ontology. One is inclined to wish a plague on both their houses. But not before exhausting certain anthropological observations, such as the absence of any necessary relation between what people do and the reasons they may have for doing it.

Intention and Convention

Eskimo are famous for customs of gift giving. "Gifts make slaves," they sometimes explain, "as whips make dogs." By contrast, a people famous for belligerence may have equally paradoxical motives for fighting. "They fought, they beat each other," writes a long-time resident among the Yanomamö of Brazil, "I don't know why; they said it was in order to be more peaceful and to be friends." There seems to be no adequate relation between the character of conventional practices, such as giving gifts or making war, and the intentions that predicate them, whether these intentions be described in social terms (e.g., gaining status) or as subjective dispositions (e.g., belligerence). The cross-cultural argument, moreover, can be supported from our own social experience. Psychoanalysis as well as common experience documents that an aggressive intent can be realized in an act of sex or on a field of football, by being excessively polite to someone, ignoring him or insulting him, by presenting a lecture or writing a book review (" that'll teach 'em"). Any given intention may correspond to an indefinite set of cultural practices, and vice versa, since the intention is connected to the convention by a relative and contextual scheme of significance.

But if the connection is arbitrary, it is not for all that aleatory, inasmuch as it is motivated within the cultural order. This would be true even if the act had unprecedented social effects. Say that gift giving established a novel form of social advancement: it would still find some logical motivation—it would "make sense"—in the culture as constituted. The disparity between conventions and intentions thus becomes a strong argument for culture as sui generis. It seems incorrect to deny that individual action is culturally determined, since this is all it can be.

The same dismal prospect appears implied by intrinsic features of symbolic consciousness and discourse. Nothing is socially known or communicated except as it is encompassed in the existing cultural order. From the first moment, experience undergoes a kind of structural co-optation: the incorporation of the percept within a concept of which the perceiver is not the author. This is Durkheim's famous "sociological epistemology." Likewise, Walker Percy remarks, "It is not enough to say that one is conscious *of* something; one is also conscious of something as *being something*." Perception is instantaneously a *re*-cognition, a matching of the percept with some received social category—"There goes a bird." Human or symbolic consciousness thus consists of acts of classification involving the subsumption of an individual perception within a social conception. Hence, as percept belongs to concept in the way that an instance belongs to its class, so does experience belong to culture.

Moreover, we know—at least since Saussure and Cassirer—that the cultural category by which experience is appropriated is for its part referentially arbitrary. It does not follow directly from the world but from a set of principled relationships between categories. The contrast in French between the terms '*fleuve*' and '*rivière*' entails a different segmentation of fluvial objects than the usual English glosses 'river' and 'stream,' inasmuch as the French distinction does not turn on relative size but on whether or not the water flows into an ocean. There is no necessary starting point for any such cultural scheme in "reality," as Stuart Hampshire writes—while noting that many philosophers have believed there is. Rather, the particular conceptual scheme or "language game" constitutes the possibilities of worldly reference for the people of a given society, even as that scheme is constructed on principled distinctions among signs which, in relation to objects, are never the only possible distinctions. It follows that there is no such thing as an immaculate perception.

The argument from symbolic discourse has the same apparent implication. Insofar as the sentence asserts, it does so by seating a specific identification within a cultural class. A sentence is minimally a grammatical subject and a predicate—"There goes a bird." The grammatical subject identifies something in particular—"[it] there." But the predicate describes it in the terms of (relative) generals—"bird," "going": once more a class whose criteria are values of the prevailing cultural scheme.

On the other hand, it is well known that in speaking the individual puts the entire cultural scheme at his own personal disposition. The famous "shifters" of discourse—the pronouns "I" and "you," adverbs of time and place ("now" and "then," "here" and "there"), tenses of the verb, etc.—contextualize all abstract categories by the speaker's reference to himself and his particular situation. Speech invents a Cartesian world, developed outward from the true and certain knowledge of the "I." In practice, the individual is the archimedean point of the cultural universe. For on the coordinates of his standpoint, hence of his interests, all of culture is transcendentally laid out, and all meanings, which without him are merely virtual or possible, become actual, referential, and intentional.

Yet here linguistics joins up with certain clear and distinct ideas of social psychology, sociology, and anthropology: the common finding that "I is another" (*Je est un autre*). Such was the point of George Herbert Mead's sustained demonstration that the self becomes known as an object by assuming the attitude of another toward one's own act or gesture: an identification with the other that alone permits reflection upon the self and to which language is indispensable. For Mead, as for Schütz, this "interchangeability of standpoints" is essential both to the origin of the self and the origin of human society. For Rousseau it was the origin of human society itself: uniquely endowed with the sentiment of *pitié* which places him in the position of the one who suffers, man begins by experiencing himself as identical to his fellows. But that too, as Benveniste teaches, is the true character of the apparently egocentric symbolic discourse.

For the "I" of speech necessarily predicates a "you," and vice versa, even as the two are always reversible. No matter how egocentrically the world is laid out in speech, "I" am never alone in it. In dialogue, "I" and "you" exchange places: referential standpoints are necessarily reversed—shall we not say?—between *us*. This interchangeability is indispensable to interpretation and communication, since without it I could not know that your "here" is my "there." It must follow that the "you" to whom I speak, and who becomes "I" in speaking to me, is in some fundamental sense like me, namely, in the capacity of social person.

The consequences, as Benveniste says, spread out in all directions. We can understand why Lévi-Strauss founds the passage from nature to culture on reciprocity as the decisive (i.e., objectified) form of overcoming the opposition of self and other. Since reciprocity in this parallels the essential characteristics of symbolic discourse, we might even credit his explanation by inherent principles of the human mind. But more consequential for present purposes are inherent qualities of human society. If there are other "I's" whose standpoints I make my own, it becomes uniquely possible for humans to constitute social universals, categories, and groups that extend indefinitely in space and time. Somewhat enigmatically, Sartre says that a city derives its reality from "the ubiquity of its absence. It is present in each one of its streets *insofar* as it is always elsewhere." The enigmas dissolve when it is recognized that the existence of other "I's," become "us," generalizes the representation from a diversity of perspectives and so determines a collective entity. Nor would Durkheim's "collective consciousness" and "collective representations" then appear so fantastic.

The interchangeability of opposed standpoints is decisive for the development of all such objectified social entities that are

likewise ubiquitous in their absence—"lineages," "governments," "nations," "humanity"—including their normative attributes. These categories cannot be merely nominal, because
even if there are only individuals they are conscious of themselves as "species beings." I have heard a Fijian elder narrate the
doings of his clan over eight generations in the first-person pro-
noun. Upon such symbolic reification rests all we call "tradition," "norm," "morality"—in brief, "a culture."

Never present as such to individual experience, the institutions
of society thus become capable of ordering subjective interests
and actions—that is, by virtue of a common membership with
"the generalized other." Nor will my purposes be completely
idiosyncratic: even when opposed to some other they are formulated on a common cultural logic. Yet this further allusion to
Mead reminds us that different values of the social logic, some
more particularistic, some more universal, intersect in the person. The individual is a social being, but we must never forget
that he is an individual social being, with a biography not the
same as that of anyone else. Here is someone to whom "attention
must be paid." For, to adopt Mead's vocabulary, if there is a
"me" that incorporates the attitude of some group at some level
of generality, there is also an "I" that retains a potential freedom
of reaction to the "generalized other." This means that life in
society is not an automatic genuflection before the superorganic
being but a continuous rearrangement of its categories in the projects of personal being. In the final section of this paper I will
describe this dialectic, which is nothing less than structural
transformation, as a symbolic process.

Dialectics of Structure and Action

The word "interest" derives from a Latin impersonal verbal
construction meaning "it makes a difference." An interest in
something is the difference it makes for someone. Happy etymol-
ogy, since it runs parallel to the Saussurean definition of conceptual value. The sign is determined as a concept by its differential relation to other signs. The meaning of "blue" is fixed by
the copresence of other terms, such as "green"; if, as is true in
many natural languages, there were no "green," the term "blue"
would have greater conceptual and referential extension. The
same goes for God the Father, a dollar bill, motherhood or filet

mignon: each has a conceptual sense according to its differential place in the total scheme of such symbolic objects. On the other hand, the symbolic object represents a differential interest to various subjects according to its place in their life schemes. "Interest" and "sense" are two sides of the same thing, the sign, as related respectively to persons and to other signs. Yet my interest in something is not the same as its sense.

Saussure's discussion of linguistic value helps make the point, as it is framed on an analogy to economic value. The value of a five-franc piece is determined by the dissimilar objects with which it can be exchanged, such as so much bread or milk, and by other units of currency with which it can be contrastively compared—one franc, ten francs. By these relationships the significance of five francs in the society is constituted. Yet this general and abstract sense is not the value of five francs *to me*. To me, it appears as a specific interest or instrumental value, and whether I buy milk or bread with it, give it away, or put it in the bank, all depends on my particular circumstances and objectives. As implemented by the subject, the conventional value acquires an intentional value, and the conceptual sense an actionable reference.

I am suggesting that the classic distinction between language and speech be expanded into an argument about culture in general: that culture likewise has a dual mode of existence. It appears both in human projects and intersubjectively as a structure or system. Intentionally arranged by the subject, it is also conventionally constituted in the society. But as a symbolic process, it is differently organized in these two dimensions.

Following Ricoeur's remarks on language, immediately we see that culture-as-lived has a different kind of phenomenal existence than culture-as-constituted. For the sign enjoys an actual being, *in praesentia*, only as it is inscribed in human action. As a scheme of relationships between symbolic categories, the "system" is merely virtual. It exists *in absentia*, in the way that the English language, as distinct from people's actual utterances, exists perfectly or as a whole only in the community as a whole. We can say that, as lived, the symbolic fact is a phenomenal "token," whose "type" is its mode of existence in culture-as-constituted. Besides, in culture-as-constituted the sign has an abstract sense, merely signifying, by virtue of all possible relations with other signs, all its possible uses; it is thus "stimulus free," not bound to any particular worldly referent. But people live in the world as well as by signs, or better, they live in the world by signs, and in action they index the conceptual sense by reference to the objects of their existence. In naive and evidently universal human experience, signs are the names of things "out there." What I am trying to say in a too fancy way was better put by an Indian recounting his experiences with the Canadian government in Ottowa: "An ordinary Indian can never see the 'government.' He is sent from one office to another, is introduced to this man and that, each of whom sometimes claims to be the 'boss,' but he never sees the real government, who keeps himself hidden."

Like Sartre's city, then, the Canadian government is the distant echo of a Kantian "community." Community is a temporally disjunctive judgment, as of a whole having many parts, which are thus comprehended as mutually determining: "as coordinated with, not subordinated to one another, not in one direction only as a series, but reciprocally as in an aggregate." Likewise culture-as-constituted is a mutual determination of significant forms, and as the significance of any given form depends on the copresence of the others—as God the Father is defined by God the Son, and vice versa—the "system" is indeed systemic on the condition that it is synchronic. Structure is a state. But action unfolds as a temporal process. And in intentional action the logic of relationship between signs lies precisely in their orientation: sequentially and consequentially, as means and ends of people's purposes. Moreover, I (and others) are constantly putting these signs in various and contingent relationships. Today I decide to humiliate someone by giving him a gift he cannot repay; no, better perhaps to call him the name he deserves; or then again, I could review his book. In structure, the sign is fixed by differential relationships to other signs; in action, it is variously combined with other signs in implicational relationships.

I have said that the sign is substantialized in action by reference to the world. But as every such context by which the sign is substantially defined is unique, so then is every individual's expression of the culture-as-constituted. Moreover, in their several projects people effect contingent relationships between signs which are not necessarily those ordained in the culture-as-constituted. Recall Mead's observations on the possible slippage between intentional values and conventional values, figured as a distinction between the "I" and the "me." Now it seems incorrect to deny that people can change their culture, since, as Mead concluded, that's all they ever do.

The two dimensions of culture are indeed mutually irreducible, but we are now in a position to show that they are dialectically interpenetrable. First, however, some ground rules. The possibility that a personal arrangement of symbolic forms will have structural effect clearly depends on many conditions of the culture-as-constituted: the improvisations that can be logically motivated, as by analogy, metaphor, or the like; the institutional freedom to do so; the position of the actor in a social hierarchy that gives his action structural weight, makes it more or less consequential for others. All such conditions vary society to society and may be empirically ascertained. But they are not here matters of theoretical principle. Here I am concerned solely with the ways—if you want, the mechanisms—by which structure and project interact as a symbolic process. I identify two such ways: the functional displacement of sign relationships in personal action, and the practical revaluation of signs in the famous "context of the situation."

Action begins and ends in structure, begins from the biography of the individual as a social being to end by the absorption of his action in a cultural practico-inert, the system-as-constituted. But if in the interim signs are functionally displaced, set into novel relationships with one another, then by definition the structure is transformed. And in this interim, the condition of the culture-as-constituted may actually amplify the consequences of an individual's action. When during the Vietnam War some young professor in a large midwestern university thought to adapt the tactics of the civil rights movement to the campus by inventing the "teach-in" on the model of the "sit-in," it politicized the academy in an unprecedented way—not envisioned, for example, by the already established "free speech" movement. It even became appropriate for middle-class students in Eastern universities to abandon their Ivy League costumes for what Tom Wolfe calls "prole gear," especially blue jeans and work shirts. The students metaphorized their changed relations to an adult bourgeois world they had once anticipated inheriting by masquerading in the symbols of society's underclasses—though work was clearly one of

because the "objective" things, as well as the social persons, thus represented in the terms of a conventional reason also have their own reasons. The world is under no obligation to correspond to the categories by which it is thought—even if, as Durkheim said, it can only exist for people in the way that it is thought. Thus, in the dialectic of culture-as-constituted and culture-as-lived, we also discover some possibility of reconciling the most profound antimony of social science theory, that between structure and practice: reconciling them, that is, in the only way presently justifiable—as a symbolic process.

4 Choice in the Spending of Time

Mary Jean Bowman
UNIVERSITY OF CHICAGO

As Von Mises said, "It is acting that provides man with the notion of time and makes him aware of the flux of time." Many facets of time elude us. Thus whether and in what sense time may be "more valuable" than in former epochs depends upon which of our relationships to time we are trying to grasp. Unquestionably, however, time is "scarcer" today in that potential uses of time have multiplied while we still have just twenty-four hours in a day.

Illumination of how decisions of individuals and households affect the allocation of ever-scarce time has come from the new microeconomics of the household and also from a new time-space human geography. Developments in the more general analysis of decision making under uncertainty also are basic. And we need to understand the absorption and economizing of time in decisions even when use of time is peripheral to the decision. Today I explore some of the gaps in our analysis of time without attempting to codify the main accomplishments of this rich array of research.

Of the Nature of Time and of Decision

Calendar or clock time is the least subjective mode of time even though it is an artifact. Clock time paces and synchronizes activities, but also it measures off time as anticipated in decisions about the future. It is against lapsed time that we sense "the speed with which time goes by," which is the other side of the perceived "duration" of an activity. Real time as subjectively experienced is an extended present in which decisions are made. Thus St. Augustine wrote of three times: the past in the present, the present in the present, and the future in the present—the trio of recollection, experience, and expectation. But recollection and

Acknowledgment is made to the Guggenheim Foundation.

49

expectation are very different: past time no longer can be altered, whereas imagined future time has many possible paths.

Time and Money   There are both close parallels and subtle differences in the ways we speak of time and of money. We speak of wasting time and wasting money; in both cases we mean bad allocation of a generalized means of "purchasing power." Likewise we think of "shortage of time" and of money almost identically. But we emphasize also that "there are things that money can't buy." A person might say "time hangs heavy on my hands," but never do we say this of money—we could literally throw money away, but we cannot get rid of time. Whether it seems to move sluggishly or quickly, time is inseparable from our being. We can "take time" or take some of our money to procure something, but to take someone else's time is quite different from picking up some of his money. We may admonish another: "take your time," don't worry about "taking" my time. We may "trade time" over time, as among student families in babysitting. But to "live on borrowed time" has an unworldly connotation not associated with "living on borrowed money." Where in the spectrum of societal types do these various usages appear?

We may "save" both time and money in the sense of using them prudently, to leave more to be dispensed for important uses—but there that analogy stops. An individual's time is a real resource, but it can be neither stored nor hoarded; it is laid out in one way or another at a rate inexorably determined by the years of our lives. Money, by contrast, though it can be used to price alternative uses of personal time, is not attached to the person; it can be stored for future use and spent at a rate we choose. Thus we come to two related concepts: that of "liquidity" and of "investment versus consumption."

Everyone learns that money is a "liquid asset"—though its value oozes away during inflation. Liquidity or the storing of money enables us to divide an act of exchange between two dates and to defer decisions until the future unfolds into the moving present. Money is little changed by the nature of those who hold title to it, whereas each man's time is unique. Nevertheless, people can be deprived of command over their time by slavery, and most of us contract to sell some of our time—whereby others come to control our potential actions.

And so, if we would speak of the "liquidity" of a person's time, we must compare not time and money but rather the ranges of potential services from human capital and physical capital. In general, human capital is much the more adaptable, but within either sort there can be capital with greater or lesser potential for diverse uses. We have a putty-clay model for physical capital, and we distinguish generalized from specialized uses of human capital. Children are in the "putty" stage of human-capital formation, and participation in general rather than early vocational training enlarges the options in later decisions, including greater adaptability to changes in labor markets. To accomplish real saving with money one must transform it into real investments. To accomplish real saving of time one invests time in the acquisition of capabilities for the uses of future time. Henry Ford is reputed to have said that "no successful boy ever saved any money; he spent it as fast as he got it for things to improve himself." With its implied allocation of time, that is the core idea in today's theory of investment in human beings.

Decisions, Uncertainty, and Sequential Dependence   The *cumulative nature* of experienced time, our open and *uncertain* views into the future, and the *irreversibility* of the flow of time—all these have profound implications for how we spend our time. From each decision, big or small, a train of consequences ensues.

When families in a traditional culture are confronted with new ways of life, the strains of decision making about time can be severe. Whether to send a daughter to school can exemplify such critical decisions; the parents' choice may be made deliberately or by default, but in either case a whole future is being chosen—for the daughter, for the daughter's daughter, and for the parents themselves. Parents may be fearful and uncertain about the effects of schooling. Moreover, time spent in school takes time away from productive contributions to the family economy, which are often substantial in less-developed societies. More difficult to quantify but clearly perceived by parents and neighbors is the foregone *learning* of those who continue in school. This is not solely a matter of what girls miss in the acquisition of traditional homemaking skills; it is also a sacrifice of time in acculturation to many traditional roles.

Casual, seemingly small, decisions can be no less important for the shaping of lives than the calculated choices among major alternatives. Moreover, uncertainty and clouded foresight may be no greater in looking toward consequences of the "big" decisions than in considering implications of day-to-day choices among activities. Successive small choices can yield cumulative consequences, with increasing returns per hour to particular ways of spending time; by our choices we acquire not merely habits but addictions—whether to drugs, to hobbies, or to work.

Sequential dependence of our choices and the increasing returns to choices pose problems in each life—problems often recognized more clearly in hindsight than at the time of decision. Furthermore, given many uncertainties, young people and their elders often will differ in their assessments of likely future outcomes of current choices. Those differences are compounded by different subjective perceptions of the lengths of the years that lie ahead.

Embedded in these human tussles with time are some problems for economic analysis. Where there are increasing returns, we cannot optimize by incremental decisions that equate alternatives at the margin; the best alternatives may lie along very different routes. Unfortunately, we cannot resolve this problem by applying a theory which assumes that people correctly anticipate effects of present choices on future sequences in uses of time and associated utilities over the span of life. How far affluence with its high relative price for time sets in train sequences of decisions along certain paths rather than quite different ones is important.

Misjudgments in the spending of time may arise from its very scarcity. In a fast-moving society we often underestimate how long a task will take; then what happens? Mumford speculated that rapid communication and close time coordination lead to "broken time and broken attention," whereas in earlier periods slower communication blocked such interferences. Does haste kill the patience needed to master an art? Or, on the contrary, does affluence encourage acquisition of skills in the pursuit of hobbies that differ from earlier crafts primarily in combining skills with more purchased goods? Are we showered with such an overload of messages that much time is soaked up in identifying which are important? Or, alternatively, do we give up that winnowing and relapse into what someone called "addled subjectivity?" These things happen variously to different people.

Perhaps "the fine art of spending time" is not keeping pace with the multiplying options for uses of time.

Freedom of Choice in the Spending of Time

When change is slow and not specifically valued for its own sake, time may be conceived in such large spans that its use does not become a focus for decision. For the small child, time can amble, unpressed by looming tomorrows and interrupted not by clock time but by "meal time" and "going-to-bed time." A sense of bounded time probably arises only as a society accepts subordination to clock time and faces coordination of tasks among crafts and workshops, requiring the synchronizing signals of bells and clocks. Merchants discovered the price of time, measuring its passage with profits, and expansion of activities in space gave them a keener perception of the duration of time. Mumford judged the clock more than the steam engine to be the key machine of industrialism.

But the reorientation of a society toward time will not occur overnight. Often in developing countries "target workers" initially respond to higher pay by working less; only with increases in available goods and expanding awareness of what money can buy does a settled wage force emerge. In many times and places it has been observed that punctuality and the time discipline of coordinated industrial activity are learned gradually.

Social Organization and Bounds on Choice   Timing by the clock reduces our autonomy, but it also can liberate. By facilitating better coordination of activities, it fine tunes our use of time and thereby augments our resources of time. Clock time also signals when we have intervals of autonomous choice among activities.

The temporal structure of modern society derives from the intersecting of activities of many individuals moving through time and space. If we merely add up the activities of individuals we miss these interactive effects, which set bounds on the possible time and space dimensions of activities. These patterns constitute the core of proliferating studies by Swedish geographers under the leadership of Torsten Hägerstrand. Their approach, which emphasizes the inseparability of time and space as a framework for human action, is eminently suited for exploring "free time" and freedom of choice in the allocation of time. As Hägerstrand

says, when a person withdraws from activity he influences the
options of others; "he ceases to be a resource for collaborative
tasks and social interaction. One individual's use of his freedom
influences what other individuals will be able to do with theirs."
In similar manner one may say that during the time when people
are hidden in planes or cars they are inaccessible at work or
home; "does more mobility above some threshold perhaps reduce productive interaction rather than increasing it?"

Even in "open" societies, activities become crowded into
selective conjunctures in space and time, which constrain choices
in the spending of time. Freedom is devoured when central controls are imposed upon "nonworking" time to ensure that uses of
so-called free time will be controlled in harmony with the "interests of the state."

The Short Run and the Long Run   Marshall's distinction between short run and long run can help us to identify "discretion-
ary" or free time. Free time is then time that has not been tied up
by prior commitments. As we shorten the time horizon, the proportions of time that could be regarded as free will diminish.

There is enormous diversity among individuals and between
societies in the extent of forward commitments and for how long
into the future. Thus an important dimension of choices in the
spending of time becomes how far and for what activities free
choices today entail future commitments and thereby constrain
future choices in the use of time. We know something about
contrasts in this respect between agrarian societies and societies
scheduled by clock and calender; however, systematic theoretical
exploration in this area is scanty.

A related question—flexibility in working hours—has attracted
considerable attention, however. Overloading of communal
facilities—such as restaurants at noon or transport at opening and
closing hours—has impelled much of this thinking. But often it is
contended also that more flexible working hours will improve the
"quality" of nonwork time—especially for women with dual responsibilities. After exploring this problem, John Owen recently
concluded that most of the "saved" time would be diverted into a
more ambitious life style but with little gain for what one would
call "leisure." He judges that possible gains from flexible work
time would be offset in three ways: (1) more labor-force partici-

pation by women, (2) residential up-grading that would neutralize potential reduction in commuting time, and (3) taking time for leisure in larger modules. Only the third suggests to me either a raise in quality of leisure time or reduction of rigidities in forward commitments of time.

The Utility of Time Spent at Work   The quality of experience at work can be a significant factor in decisions about allocation of time between work and other activities. This fact has not been ignored in economics though it has been neglected in applications of the modern economic theory of the allocation of time.

Consider what has happened to usage of the word "work." With advancing technology, people more often leave their homes for employment, a transformation that has generated the strange definition of "work" that counts only work done away from home. An amorphous residual of "nonwork" includes washing the kitchen floor, eating a meal, and going to the theater. Division of time between work and other activities seems tidy so long as we do not press questions as to what determines the decisions that people make with respect to even this gross division of their time. But the closer we come to models of utility maximization (or even to preference orderings) in microeconomic theory about allocation of time, the more problems we encounter relating to definition and interpretation of uses of time. In all the real moments that make up our lives we are having direct experiences, not merely chugging away like machines to turn out something that will appear only in the future. Adam Smith wrote of compensations in pay related to the unattractiveness of a job, an idea more recently expressed as "equalizing differences." Oscar Lange's theory of democratic socialism explicitly postulated freedom to choose how one will spend his working life, with appropriate adjustments in pay. Rarely, however, have manpower planners admitted such considerations into their models.

The quality of the time that we spend in one activity or another depends both on what we are doing and on the surroundings of our activity. Many of the purchased inputs into our consumption take the form of services; how many of those services yield satisfaction not only to the recipients but also to those whose time is spent in performing the services? Contrast domestic service with professional service. Today some of us may deplore the "servant shortage," but the other side of the same story is better opportunities for many who formerly would have become servants—all part of the democratization of affluence. Services that challenge individuals to use their capabilities and imagination account for a growing fraction of the labor force and for a still larger fraction of working time.

Looking across labor markets, we observe a trade-off between limited but rigid hours of work and greater autonomy in work but longer time at work. Today it is individuals with most control over how they spend working time who put in the longest hours—and from their ranks come those who devote the most hours to community service. Wilbert Moore concluded that "it is only when the scarcity of time is a problem that its use is likely to be consistent with personal creativity and socially approved values."

The Old and the Young in an Affluent Society

The modern economic theory of the allocation of time has been applied almost exclusively to persons in the active working years. The old mostly have been ignored, and the time of the young is considered only in terms of foregone earnings as a cost of education. These two populous categories have in common a low market value for their time in a society in which the market value of human time generally has been rising.

Poverty and Surplus of Time among the Old   The affluent society is not gentle with the elderly, who have even more need than adolescents for time-intensive services from the active population. The "problem of the elderly" is not solely one of their demographic proportion; relative prices of many material goods may be falling, but prices of services they need are another matter. Furthermore, all the pressures that make time scarcer relative to claims on it among active adults further reduce opportunities for old people either to collaborate in work or for informal association. And so we face both desocialization of the elderly and rising requirements for redistributive payments to them.

Options for use of time among the elderly are shrunk, then, by low income, by limited chance to work for pay, and by need for expensive services. In addition, the structure of our economy and the pace we set in many activities bears down hard on them and depreciates the value of their time. We deprive them of the satisfaction of performing services of at least some value to others, and we are too greedy with our time to accord them dignity and self-respect.

Children Are People Too   The young, unlike the old, have futures: distinctly in the minds of their elders and gradually in their own. Having futures, they have value, and it is to their futures that most of the economic analysis of investments in education has been directed. The allocation of children's time receives attention primarily from this perspective, which incorporates as an important explanatory factor in educational decisions the low or high value of children's time in productive activities that they forego when attending school. The high value of adult time in the labor market—itself partly a result of rising education among the working population—is an incentive to continuing investment in schooling of children who have comparatively low current potentials for earning but high potential value of time concentrated on learning. Recognition of the value of childrens' learning time has stimulated the introduction of the concept of opportunity cost into pedagogical research about allocations of the in-school time of children—not only as planned by the teacher but also as displayed by the children themselves.

It seems sometimes that in economics we view children just as raw material inputs for the production of another product (which, however, is never finished), namely, their future selves. We sometimes consider them as a component of their parents' consumption, but rarely as final consumers in their own right. Even more rarely do we ask what adults can learn from children. Children are people too, and within their own worlds they too are choosing how they will spend their time.

These are worlds that adults may enlarge or shrink, but can fully control only by destruction of a human spirit. The nature of our interventions, whether by intent or by neglect, can never be taken for granted.

In our time-conscious society, are we pressing their mortality upon children with a frenetic organization of their time? Are the days passing when for children, at least, time might sometimes "go to sleep in the afternoon sunshine?" What are the implications of the fact that for most children the countryside is accessible only as a special project?

The rise in the relative value of labor-market time of women

5 Prudent Aspirations for Social Inquiry

Lee J. Cronbach
STANFORD UNIVERSITY

Each anniversary has its own mood. The celebrants may be proud of the honoree's long reign and foresee further triumphs, or the occasion may be only a routine marker in a stable, productive career. Sometimes the proud days are long past, and there are only memories to celebrate. In social science today the mood is equivocal. The profession is proud of much work old and new and of the influence social inquiry has had, yet is troubled that little theory cumulates and distressed that many recommended practical actions fail. The persons most disappointed are the ones in the profession and in the world of action who hoped that our conclusions would directly indicate what social policy should be. Findings of social science can rarely or never identify "right" courses of action. Fortunately, today's profession is coming to see the rationalist, scientistic ideal as no more than an infantile dream of omnipotence. The present mood, one hopes, bespeaks an institution on the brink of adulthood, ready to claim a role within its capabilities and aware that waiting for its Newton is as pointless as waiting for Godot.

Expressions of this newfound prudence come from all corners of the field. Even a severely selective bibliography must mention Aaron (1978), Bronfenbrenner (1979), Campbell (1974), Cole (et al. 1979), Coleman (1972), Glass (1979), Lindblom and Cohen (1979), McGuire (1973), Meehl (1970, 1971, 1978), Myrdal (1973), Nelson (1977), Rivlin (1974), Simon (1969), and Weiss (1977). Writing almost independently, these economists, psychologists, sociologists, and political scientists addressed different audiences. The time has come for the whole of social science to hear the voices as the chorus they are.

I thank Donald Campbell, Philip Converse, William Kruskal, D. C. Phillips, David Rogosa, and Richard E. Snow for comments that led to many changes from the paper originally delivered. But I have retained some of the thoughts that one or another of them questioned.

Recent social science has sacrificed to false idols. The 1960s and early 1970s placed faith in sheer technique. Psychologists—many of them—came to think that testing of null hypotheses is sufficient to make a science and that randomized field tests are sufficient to determine a policy. (See the adverse comments of MacKenzie 1977; Meehl 1967; and Pillemer and Light 1979). Sociologists, newly enamored of path analysis, began earnestly to give causal meaning to correlations. Economists, despite their greater experience, began to see that same kind of analysis as a servomechanism with which to move the world. It was in those years that the "best and brightest" decided to put not only the Pentagon but all federal services under rational management, and invited social scientists into the corridors of power.

Sometimes we speak as if the social scientists' quest for theoretical understanding and the quest for information of immediate relevance are separate missions, but the two are not separable. The distinction refers not to the form of the work or its fruit but only to the payoff function the investigators apply to their own work—especially the rate at which each one discounts the future. Decisions are influenced by concepts the theoreticians put forward, and studies initiated for short-run purposes can start a fermentation from which large new ideas will be distilled. The critical literature to which I have referred is concerned with so-called basic research as well as with research overtly oriented to policy; both kinds of study face the same epistemological difficulties. The recent attempt to meet short-run demands through targeted inquiry, however, is instructive enough to receive special attention.

The new rationalism idealized rigor. In the best of all polities, it was thought, cost-benefit printouts bunched in the fists of undersecretaries and legislators would beat down ill-considered initiatives. Goals of organizations and actions would at last be made explicit. Then numerical measures of goal attainment would expose any default or slackness to condemnation. Sound social-science techniques were held up as an oracle; an appeal to inquiry would reveal the right action, with respect to each problem in turn. The Arrow theorem might never have been.

Eagerness to replace political contention and accommodation with scientific authority has a long history. As far back as Condorcet, social scientists were claiming the right and duty to serve as Platonic Governors. At the turn of this century Albion Small, prime mover in the social sciences at the University of Chicago, was one of the many who expected society to take its direction from academe. Research would tell elected officials what to think and how to act. The academic social scientist was to be "sailing master" for the ship of state (Small 1910, p. 277). Small did see social affairs as complex and value laden and cherished no ideal of objectivity. Quite the contrary, he wished the Institute of Social Scientists to become a moral elite whose consensus on values would determine the social course (Christakes 1978; Small 1910, esp. pp. 237 ff.). Activism waxes and wanes and waxes again. In the generation after Small, and again in that after Lewin, social scientists cherishing academic respectability retreated into work safely remote from affairs (Lynd 1939; Lyons 1969; Sanford 1970).

Around 1970, an activist surge held out high hopes for an "experimenting society" (Campbell 1969b; Rivlin 1971; Schultze 1968). Preferably, the thesis ran, government would be able to delay action until a tough-minded field trial had shown the effectiveness of a proposed innovation; post hoc studies are untrustworthy as well as untimely. But there would be a precious opportunity for learning in even a retrospective attempt to appraise an innovation.

The brilliant New Jersey welfare study was one of the first attempts to answer a large policy question by experiment. Its difficulties, plus those of the Follow Through Planned Variations study, did much to deflate the expectations for empirical policy research (Aaron 1978; Levitan and Wurzburg 1979; Rivlin 1974). Meanwhile, however, we had a decade of propaganda for randomized, large-scale social experiments. Even now the grandiosity persists; one current writer tells us that two million dollars and three years is the *minimum* reasonable investment to study a proposal for educational charge (Schutz 1979).

It is a bit unfair to identify any person with the hyperbolic claims, since the writer who overstates in one paper talks sense in another. But overstatement has been plentiful. The scientistic are prone to say that experiments are convincing beyond dispute; one quote runs that "when you get an experimental result you have to believe it whether you want to or not" (relayed approvingly by Crain and York 1976, p. 252). More cautious enthusiasts say merely that the experiment is "closer to being definitive than . . . any other method of evaluating" (Rossi 1979, p. 31). In several papers (e.g., Gilbert et al. 1975), Gilbert and Mosteller condemned field tests that lack a formal comparison of the program's clients with an equivalent untreated control group. The noncomparative trial is mere "fooling around with people," having no evidential value. Such a trial will suffice, they said, if the intervention has a "slam-bang" effect. But, they went on, a change in social services usually has a small and undependable effect, and only a randomized experiment will give a valid appraisal.

Unfortunately, randomization almost always comes at the expense of representativeness. The controlled trial requires compliant agencies or volunteer subjects—both atypical. In the attempt to standardize delivery and to prevent self-selection (into or out of the program), the service may be artificialized to the point where it bears no resemblance to a practical, large-scale operation. In the propaganda for stringent comparative studies, representativeness is disparaged; Campbell (1969a) once went so far as to say that representativeness "should be removed even from our philosophy of science."

The counterargument, increasingly recognized by Campbell himself (Cook and Campbell 1979), is that matters are too complex for firm quantitative comparisons of alternative courses of action.[1] This is true of broad social programs, and of specific strategies for teaching classes or conducting psychotherapy or changing public attitudes. Random experiments are indeed welcome when they bear on the relevant question and the analysis takes into account the uncontrollable nonuniformities of treatment delivery. But a summary estimate of the "value" of a treatment should be suspect (Pillemer and Light 1979).

Plaza Sésamo, the Mexican adaptation of *Sesame Street*, had one of the world's neater experimental evaluations (Diaz-Guerrero et al. 1976). Children in three day-care centers were divided randomly, and the experimental subjects watched 130 of the educational telecasts. During each of these sessions, class-

1. To be sure, physical scientists face equal complexities. But most of their relationships are comparatively stable over generations, and many of the processes can be isolated for study in reproducible laboratory conditions.

mate controls viewed noneducational programs in another room. By the end of the year, the experimental group had piled up an unmistakable intellectual advantage. A second study used a similar design on a large scale with less-artificial conditions. Subjects given *that* year of exposure to *Plaza Sésamo* did little or no better than their control group. A plausible explanation is that the natural viewing conditions of the second study allowed more distractions. In the first study, the presence of extra observers had subtly enforced discipline. The first experiment was valid but irrelevant to practical intervention.

A minimal research report sticks to the past tense, claiming to be no more than a record of concrete particular events. But the social scientist almost invariably offers a conclusion worded in the present tense. Any such nonhistorical sentence generalizes beyond the operations of the study. The statement purports to be lawlike, to describe regularities. Popper (1961 p. 62), arguing that social laws are indeed possible, offered the example "power corrupts." Even one instance does prove that corruption can be a concomitant of access to power. That warning is worthwhile knowledge but hardly lawlike. One counterinstance—and I believe there have been some—is sufficient to infirm an unqualified power-corruption law. To approach a believable present-tense generalization one must tease out the circumstances that make corruption likely (as Popper recognized).

To formulate a would-be generalization properly, one has to recognize particular objects or systems as members of a class, to observe some of those objects, and on that basis make an assertion about the class. A crucial part of the task is to bound the class of systems to which the summary purportedly applies. I shall be brief on this point, as the matter has been much discussed (Cole et al. 1979; Cronbach 1975, 1976, 1978; Myrdal 1973; Popper 1961; Simon 1969).

A social system consists of the persons who affect each other, hence the unit to be observed is an institution, a community, or a nation. Consequently, the number of units independently treated is usually small and statistical inference is weak. To treat individuals one a at time, as in the laboratory, builds up the sample size; but the treatment is then remote from *social* science. The small and short-lived groups of laboratory social psychology are equally remote from a science of society. An event in a community is likely to interact with other features of the social scene. For students of an innovation to speak of an effect "of the treatment" is therefore shortsighted. The circumstances surrounding the intervention are part of the cause (Mackie 1974).

The New Jersey welfare payments went to widely separated households; readiness to seek a job under that condition perhaps forecast nothing about an operational program (Rivlin 1974). In a real program, payments would go to all eligibles. Then communication among neighbors could easily alter the norms for work response.

In Iraq in the 1920s, the British put down a tribal insurrection by saturation bombing of a few villages—truly a slam-bang effect. The observation was generalized by the British into a principle: the way to use air power is area bombing (Wilensky 1967). In World War II, Allied raiders over Germany acting on that principle suffered heavy losses. The bombs did not stop war production, and they probably stiffened the will to resist; the Reich was not a tribal village.

Social knowledge is used in circumstances other than those originally studied. New sites and new clienteles have to be served, and the original site changes with time. Extrapolation is speculative even when the effect is established beyond question in the original context. Therefore, the interpreter should always question whether an observed effect is transportable and how much the ostensible cause depends for its effect on contextual factors.

Disregard of causally relevant conditions is inherent in all the time-hallowed invocations of ceteris paribus. Post hoc matching, partialing, and covariance adjustment try to tell us what relations would become if we could wipe out certain correlations of background factors with events. In evaluations of treatments, these adjustments seek to describe a counterfactual world in which initial characteristics of persons do not influence the treatment they get (Meehl 1970, 1971, 1978). To create such a world would require intervention radical enough to denature the treatment.

One of Meehl's examples is the finding that those who participated in high-school extracurricular activities tended to be more successful after graduation. Social status correlates with success and with participation, so eager methodologists partial it out. They think they learn what will happen when low SES students enter as many activities as highs do. But how will this new world be created? Must lows be persuaded to abandon after-school jobs, or to withdraw time from study? Will they be paid to participate? Will participation quotas by SES levels be imposed? Or will activities be assigned to a regular school period, with attendance mandatory? Each move has a causal effect about which present data can say nothing.

Discussion of adjustments has centered particularly on attempts to compare social programs that serve dissimilar samples of clients. It is sensible to study any program in its own terms. How graduates of a training program fare is a proper question; administrators can be satisfied or dissatisfied with the answer, and if dissatisfied can search for plausible reasons. Program comparison enters the realm of fantasy, however, when the client groups that alternative programs are able to attract and hold are not equivalent. Brilliant work has been done recently to refine the analysis of structural-equation models. (See separate reviews by Bentler and Woodward 1979; and by Heckman 1976.) These advances should increase the yield from field data, but I cannot share the optimism that superadjustments will warrant causal conclusions. Curve fitting cannot lift us into orbit unless fueled by substantive insight.

There is an old University of Chicago story that when the Cowles Commission moved into the Social Science Research Building someone invited Professor Thurstone upstairs to see their pioneering approach to econometrics. Thurstone inspected the models, the arrows, the equation systems. Someone mentioned that the key to solution of the equations was the insertion of zeros to dispose of relations that prevailing economic theory regarded as negligible. Thurstone admired the elegance but added sadly that the scheme would never do for psychology. "In psychology," he said, "we never know where to put the zeroes."

Quite apart from the logical difficulties that arise from ceteris paribus statements, conventional correction procedures fly in the face of some almost elementary mathematical truths. Technical detail is out of place here, but an emerging line of thought does require mention. The strength of a quantitative relationship in a subpopulation will usually differ from that in the parent population and from that in some other subpopulation. Karl Pearson established that principle before 1910,[2] but only recently have social scientists awakened to the message of his mathematics for their work. The story has now been told in various forms by statisticians, econometricians, and psychometric specialists in education (Cochran and Rubin 1973; Heckman 1976; Reichardt, in Cook and Campbell 1979).

We study population 1, but often we want a conclusion about a population 2. (One population may or may not be a subset of the other.) In extending a conclusion beyond the persons and settings sampled, the obvious step is to characterize the original cases and sites and the new ones on the same variables, and to use a regression function to predict average outcome in the new population.

The variant of Pearson's conclusion that I shall refer to as "the formula" derives from a model which indicates how selection biases the extrapolation (see appendix to this paper). The formula is heuristic only, as some key terms cannot be observed. Still it is clear that, for nearly all possible values of those terms, the trend line that relates outcomes to initial conditions in population 1 will not match the trend line in population 2. Extrapolation by regression will, with few exceptions, give an incorrect forecast. The formula offers one consolation, but only to those who think that treatment effects do not depend on conditions. If two treatments respond in just the same way to changes in subjects and settings, the trend lines relating outcome to any initial measure will be parallel in equivalent samples from population 1, and the difference in mean outcomes will be the same in both populations.

In December 1979, after I had drafted the foregoing paragraphs, fortunate chance led me to a paper in econometrics that gave me pause. I amended this paper before its oral delivery just sufficiently to acknowledge that events had moved beyond my ken. Since then, with some guidance from James Heckman, Zvi Griliches, and David Rogosa, I have run down a surprising number of relevant papers and manuscripts, some several years

2. Pearson's theorem has been routinely used by personnel psychologists to correct correlations "for restriction of range." For example, the correlation of an admission test with subsequent grades can be determined only for students admitted; the predictive validity of the test over the whole range of applicants is inferred by formula.

old, of which nearly everyone outside economics was unaware in 1979. And I have done enough exploratory investigation to gain some feeling for the methods being proposed. (The most approachable of the published papers are those of Griliches, Hall, and Hausman 1978; Heckman 1979; and Maddala 1977.)

These papers cast a new light—perhaps a rosier one—on the problems of extrapolation. My pessimistic paragraphs above, the ones originally drafted, are in line with the literature in statistics and the psychological sources on quasi-experiments; it was concluded that extrapolation is almost certain to be wrong unless one can specify rather fully the differences between populations 1 and 2. Now the econometricians suggest that often one can validly estimate how Y is related to any X in population 2 on the basis of population 1 data. The method is limited to linear relations, but it can consider X's in combination. All that is necessary is that one know how the populations differ on each X. If some X has not been observed in population 2, a distribution can be postulated. Unlike traditional extrapolation, the new approach does not envision that what was found in population 1 will be found in population 2. On the contrary, one or another algorithm is used to allow for the distorting effects of selection on the X variables and the unspecified selection that may have occurred on other variables. This seems close to magic on the first encounter and on all later encounters.

The magic, of course, lies in the assumptions. The fundamental assumption is that within any one treatment the relation under investigation is linear and not interactive. This is the same treacherous assumption required to justify extrapolation to population 2 from a randomized experiment in population 1. It amounts to assuming that all relevant causal factors operate in the same way, with the same strength, at all levels of the X variables. Additional assumptions are made about the shape of the distributions of certain variables that were not observed. Making strong assumptions is perhaps not unsuitable as a tactical first step. But the vulnerability of the methods lies in the assumptions and in various difficulties of estimation that arise. Violation of the assumptions may throw the results off entirely, and there is no way to establish, from the data collected on a sample from population 1, how far wrong the assumptions are.

The jury is still out of the practical promise of these procedures. If nothing else, the fact that the conclusion reached often differs radically from that of a conventional analysis will encourage circumspect interpretation. Even when the new methods do what they purport to do, we will never be certain how good is the forecast of the relationship in population 2. We are subject to a principle familiar in all sciences: if you assume a linear relationship, extrapolation becomes hazardous when the phenomenon is to any degree nonlinear and the reach of the extrapolation is long.

All this begins to suggest that general, lasting, definite "laws" are in principle beyond the reach of social science, that sheer empirical generalization is doomed as a research strategy. Extrapolation to new circumstances apparently has to rest on a rhetorical argument, one that relies on *qualitative* beliefs about the processes at work in the old and new situations (Campbell 1974; Meehl 1971).

In protesting against this view, some of our colleagues are beginning to sound like a kind of Flat Earth Society. They tell us that the world is essentially simple: most social phenomena are adequately described by linear relations; one-parameter scaling can discover coherent variables independent of culture and population; and inconsistencies among studies of the same kind will vanish if we but amalgamate a sufficient number of studies (e.g., Glass 1976, but see also Glass 1979; Rasch 1961; Schmidt et al. 1979).

Amalgamation can indeed suppress variation. Our data are rarely refined enough for a single study to provide convincing evidence of nonlinearity. Trends are unlikely to be uniform over disparate studies; therefore, nonlinearities are blurred when studies are amalgamated unless these are strict replications. Our "straight arrow" friends, however, are playing a losing game in defending a null hypothesis. As Anderson (1977) has shown, an investigator with substantive insight can find orderly interactions in data that the naked eye and a blunt χ^2 test call linear. Kuhn (1978, p. 219) was speaking of all sciences when he said, "To discover quantitative regularity, one must normally know what regularity one is seeking and one's instruments must be designed accordingly; even then nature may not yield generalizable results without a struggle."

The Flat Earth folk seek to bury any complex hypothesis with an empirical bulldozer. One lively contention in my field, for example, has been that an aptitude score means different things in different demographic groups. The usual study plots school marks or rated job performance against test scores, separately for males and females and for blacks and whites. If predictions are *not* conditioned by background, it is said, the trend lines for the groups should coincide even when the test means differ. If the trend line for group A lies above that for all the competitors together, however, ranking by test score undervalues the A's and in that sense is unfair. In studies of such trend lines, the disparities observed are small (Linn 1978). A solid generalization has been established, say Flat Earthians: the hypothesis implicating group background can be dismissed, and research can stop (Schmidt et al. 1973).

But this null hypothesis is logically doomed. It speaks of fallible observed scores rather than of the underlying variables. Long-familiar postulates about random error imply that thorough measures and sketchy measures of the same latent variable will exhibit different trend lines. If the population trend lines coincide for a forty-item test, they will not coincide when twenty items are used, or one hundred (Linn and Werts 1971). Shortening a test puts members of the lower-scoring group more nearly abreast of their competitors. At best, the alleged generalization is a report on current predictors (and one that ignores the message of the formula regarding data from selected groups). Even if regressions coincide for certain present tests, substantive boundary conditions that promise such a happy result would have to be discovered to justify forecasting the fairness of a new test or of an application of an old test in a new setting. Lacking validated boundary conditions, we have no logical alternative to comparing the actual regressions in each new situation.

Skepticism regarding generalizations that reach beyond time, place, and population expresses a constructive attitude, not nihilism. The sooner all social scientists are aware that data never speak for themselves, that without a carefully framed statement of boundary conditions generalizations are misleading or trivially vague, and that forecasts depend on substantive conjectures, the sooner will social science be consistently a source of enlightenment. Critics of social scientism are coming to agree about the function our profession should try to serve.

Our main stock in trade is not prescriptions or laws or definitive assessments of proposed actions; we supply concepts, and these alter perceptions (Lindblom and Cohen 1979; Rein 1976; Weiss 1977). Fresh perceptions suggest new paths for action and alter the criteria for assessment. For example, recent findings have altered perceptions of poverty in the United States (Aaron, 1978). The poor we have with us always, but not the same poor. Households move out of poverty each year; others fall into it. These economic changes are closely linked to changes in family composition. What to do about poverty becomes a different question as a result of such observations. On another subject, whether to group students by ability has been much debated among educators. Comparative experiments have generated only confusion. Now Webb (1978) demonstrates that the question is meaningless until reframed to consider whether and how students will interact in the work group.

Social scientists have complained because their knowledge is given no special status in the decision-making process. But, as Lindblom and Cohen (1979) say, we should expect the short-term decisions of the community to be much influenced by folklore, tradition, personal experience, and established beliefs. Personal transactions, as in a market, produce de facto decisions. Decisions are shaped by all those on board, not handed down from the captain's bridge. The polity moves not to a solution but toward an acceptable accommodation among conflicting interests and beliefs. The polity "satisfices" (Blumer 1971; de Jouvenel 1963; Lindblom 1965).

Concepts contribute to pluralistic decision making by helping participants examine their situations and values. Concepts are readily accepted, because parties can capitalize on them in their own ways. Quasi-prescriptive conclusions, on the other hand, invite disbelief. An assertion about what an action will lead to rests on an argument that embodies many presumptions. Credibility is for the hearer to judge. For this and other reasons, a research conclusion is likely to have little influence on the near-term fate of whatever program or site is directly examined (Cronbach and associates 1980).[3] The conclusion does feed into the evolution of aspirations and plans for action.

The social scientist helps not by playing expert but by playing

3. Conclusions are, however, directly influential in the special case where the inquiry is commissioned by an officer who exercises full command over the enterprise studied.

educator, eternally pressing the question, "Have you taken X and Z into account?" Social science is cumulative not in possessing ever-more-refined answers about fixed questions but in possessing an ever-richer repertoire of questions. The educative influence of a piece of research may extend far into the future. Concepts have enduring value, and so does a sense of what-connects-to-what.

Empirical generalizations about the strength and even the direction of relations become obsolete. As Rescher expressed it in 1970 (p. 156), social conclusions are rooted "in *transitory regularities*, deriving from . . . temporally restricted technological or institutional patterns." Simon (1976, p. 146) makes the same point: with human institutions "theory is no more likely to remain invariant over time than the theory of bridge design."

As of ten years ago, Rescher's solution to the problem of prediction was to rely on expert judgment. It is increasingly clear, however, that delegation to experts is acceptable only where all those who share power agree about values (for one of many statements on this, see Ezrahi [1980]). As of ten years ago, Simon's solution (1969) was to develop a technology of redesigning actions to fit each new set of circumstances. Even business decisions, which Simon had in mind, are hard to capture in an information technology (Keen and Morton 1978), and design for social innovations is even less likely to be highly technological. In any designing, only a small part of the work is done at a drafting table or computer terminal. The designer is obligated to interact with clients to learn their wishes and to tell them what is realizable. The designer has to acquaint himself with the site. He has to envision processes and details and to verify the practical and political viability of the proposals. This means a great deal of testing and tinkering, a research activity that will continue, as Simon noted, after the designed scheme is in place. Much of the task, then, requires on-line engagement.

But what about inquiry more detached from action? What research styles and objectives follow from the intent to advance understanding? A mixed strategy is called for: censuses and laboratory experiments, managerial monitoring and anthropological *Einfühlung*, mathematical modeling and unstructured observation. A few maxims can be offered even for eclectic social science.

Social inquiry reports on events in one or more sites during one slice of time. It can be viewed best as quantitatively assisted history. The more the observer learns of detail and process, the better; observation from afar is impoverished. The impersonal, predesigned research study is of precious little use in gaining a new idea (Glaser and Strauss 1967), however useful it may be in confirmatory research and in routine monitoring. Though one may "lose objectivity" by appearing on the scene and attending to variables not specified in advance, the benefit outweighs the loss.

I have referred to Webb's study on learning in groups. Webb created teams of students experimentally, some of uniform ability, some of deliberately mixed ability. The statistics on the predesigned comparisons were little better than chaotic. I doubt that even a much larger study would have shown any interesting relations for the design variables. It was when Webb went back to tape recordings of the teams at work that the evidence took on a sensible shape. It became clear that forming a group of mixed ability was not "the treatment." The students created their own treatment. Some groups worked collaboratively, the abler members being determined to aid the less able. These teams did well on average; their weaker members profited from help, and the abler members learned more than counterparts in other groups who did no teaching. In psychology, at least, it is often true that the juiciest harvest is the hypotheses the data suggest, not the hypotheses "under test."

External as well as internal process is important. Psychology has for too long considered the normal social unit to be one person opposite a faceless experimenter. Other disciplines have been too ready to study single institutions or single interventions. Units should be broad enough to encompass whatever community processes influence the phenomenon (Cole et al. 1979; Cronbach 1976). Understanding an adolescent's experience or that of a recipient of plural social services seems to require a community-wide ecological perspective (Bronfenbrenner 1979; Wicker 1979). Even though an educational study, for example, may have to concentrate on classrooms, classroom events are influenced by the community, the school structure, and events in the home, and the investigator will enrich his interpretation by acquainting himself with the context in which his limited unit is embedded.

Let me put it differently. All social scientists are engaged in case studies. The 1980 census is no less a case study than is Erikson's *Young Man Luther* (1958). The observations take meaning from their time and place, and from the conceptions held by those who pose the questions and decide how to tabulate. The significance of the report is slight or transient unless attention is drawn to processes that, in later days or other circumstances, will affect social outcomes.

In offering a prudent (but prideful) aspiration for social science I cannot do better than quote Prewitt's recent testimony (1980, p. 3): "The complexities of the problems for which the social and behavioral sciences might be helpful are always going to be one step ahead of the problem-solving abilities of those sciences.... They are sciences whose progress is marked, and whose usefulness is measured, less by the achievement of consensus or the solving of problems than by a refinement of debate and a sharpening of the intelligence upon which collective management of human affairs depends."

APPENDIX: TECHNICAL NOTE ON THE FORMULA

This memorandum is necessarily succinct. The derivation would be similar to that for closely related formulas given by Cronbach et al. (1977) and by Lawley (1943–44). The former source focused on the bias in estimating the main effect for treatments when two treatments are given to nonequivalent groups. Many recent papers on this theme are summarized by Reichardt in Cook and Campbell (1979). The same issues, as encountered in another guise in econometrics, are developed by Heckman (1976) and Maddala (1977).

We consider the outcome Y of a single treatment. It is assumed that the causal relations generating Y scores do not differ from population 1 to population 2. The diagram depicts the specification equations from which the formula is derived.

The variables P, D, and W describe persons at the time treatment begins. P is the ideal predictor of Y, the weighted combination of initial characteristics that completely captures the relevant information. The disturbance E'' is in principle unpredictable from characteristics of the person. D is the discriminant. The probability that a person in population 2 enters population 1 is a function of D; no other initial variable can improve the prediction of group membership. W is an arbitrarily chosen predictor. The correlations among P, D, and W may take on any mutually consistent values.

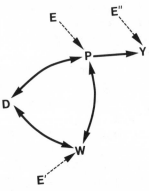

The linear equation that best describes the relation of Y to W is:

$$\hat{Y}_P = \alpha + \beta_{YP}\beta_{PD}\mu_D + \beta_{YP} \times \beta_{PD}\beta_{WD}\sigma_D^2 + \beta_{WE}\sigma_E^2 \times (W_P - \beta_{WD}\mu_D)$$
$$\beta_{WD}^2\sigma_D^2 + \beta_{W(E)}^2\sigma_E^2 + \sigma_{E'}^2$$

It is assumed that σ_E^2 and $\sigma_{E'}^2$ are uniform over the populations; σ_D^2 and μ_D may change from one population the other. The regression coefficients in the formula are those for population 1. A multivariate normal distribution of Y, P, and W in population 2 is a sufficient condition for the formula.

Under any of the following conditions, the means of W and Y in population 2 fall on the linear regression that fits population 1: (1) $\beta_{PD \cdot W} = 0$. (2) $\beta_{YP} = 0$. (3) $\mu_{D(1)} = \mu_{D(2)}$.

Under any of the following conditions, β_{YW} is the same in both populations: (1) $\beta_{PD \cdot W} = 0$. (2) $\beta_{YP} = 0$. (4) $\sigma_{D(1)} = \sigma_{D(2)}$. (5) $\beta_{WD} = 0$.

The argument can be extended readily to studies with multiple treatments by introducing a notation that allows each treatment to have its own population 1, its own P and D, and possibly a distinct W. In such a comparison one would ordinarily want to estimate regressions for all treatments in the same population 2.

REFERENCES

Aaron, Henry J. *Politics and the Professors: The Great Society in Perspective*. Washington, D.C.: Brookings Institution, 1978.

Anderson, Norman. "Weak Inference with Linear Models." *Psychological Bulletin* 84 (1977):1155–70.

Bentler, Peter M., and Woodward, J. Arthur. "Nonexperimental Evaluation Research: Contributions of Causal Modeling." In L.-E. Datta and R. Perloff (eds.), *Improving Evaluations*. Beverly Hills, Calif.: Sage Publications, 1979.

Blumer, Herbert. "Social Problems as Collective Behavior." *Social Problems* 18 (1972):298–306.

Bronfenbrenner, Urie. *The Ecology of Human Development: Experiments by Nature and Design.* Cambridge, Mass.: Harvard University Press, 1979.

Campbell, Donald T. "Prospective: Artifact and Control." In R. Rosenthal and R. L. Rosnow (eds.), *Artifact in Behavorial Research.* New York: Academic Press, 1969. (a).

Campbell, Donald T. "Reforms as Experiments." *American Psychologist* 24 (1969):409–29. (b).

Campbell, Donald T. "Qualitative Knowing in Action Research." Occasional paper. Stanford Evaluation Consortium, Stanford, Calif., 1974.

Christakes, George. *Albion W. Small.* Boston: G. K. Hall & Co., 1978.

Cochran, W. G., and Rubin, D. B. "Controlling Bias in Observational Studies: A Review." *Sankhya* 35, ser. A (1973):417–46.

Cole, Michael; Hood, Lois; and McDermott, Ray. *Ecological Niche Picking: Ecological Invalidity as an Axiom of Experimental Cognitive Psychology.* New York: Laboratory of Comparative Human Cognition, Rockefeller University, 1979.

Coleman, James S. *Policy Research in the Social Sciences.* Morristown, N.J.: General Learning Press, 1972.

Cook, Thomas D., and Campbell, Donald T. *Quasi-Experimentation: Design and Analysis Issues for Field Settings.* Chicago: Rand McNally, 1979.

Crain, Robert L., and York, Robert L. "Evaluating a Successful Program: Experimental Method and Academic Bias." *School Review* 84 (1976):233–54.

Cronbach, Lee J. "Beyond the Two Disciplines of Scientific Psychology." *American Psychologist* 30 (1975):116–27.

Cronbach, Lee J. "Research on Classrooms and Schools: Formulation of Questions, Design, and Analysis." Occasional paper. Stanford Evaluation Consortium, Stanford University, Calif., 1976.

Cronbach, Lee J. "Designing Educational Evaluations." Occasional paper. Stanford Evaluation Consortium, Stanford University, Calif., 1978. Rev. ed. San Francisco: Jossey-Bass, 1982.

Cronbach, Lee J., and associates. *Toward Reform in Program Evaluation*. San Francisco: Jossey-Bass, 1980.

Cronbach, Lee J.; Rogosa, David R.; Floden, Robert E.; and Price, Gary G. "Analysis of Covariance in Nonrandomized Experiments: Parameters Affecting Bias." Occasional paper. Stanford Evaluation Consortium, Stanford University, Calif., 1977.

de Jouvenel, Bertrand. *The Pure Theory of Politics*. Cambridge: Cambridge University Press, 1963.

Diaz-Guerrero, Rogelio, et al. "Plaza Sésamo in Mexico: An Evaluation." *Journal of Communication* 26 (1976):145–54.

Erikson, Erik H. *Young Man Luther: A Study in Psychoanalysis and History*. New York: W. W. Norton & Co., 1958.

Ezrahi, Yaron. "From Utopian to Pragmatic Rationalism: A Comparative Study in the Political Context of Scientific Advice." *Minerva*, vol. 18, no. 1 (Spring 1980).

Gilbert, John P.; Light, Richard J.; and Mosteller, Frederick. "Assessing Social Innovations: An Empirical Base for Policy." In C. A. Bennett and A. A. Lumsdaine (eds.), *Evaluation and Experiment*. New York: Academic Press, 1975.

Glaser, Barney G., and Strauss, Anselm L. *The Discovery of Grounded Theory: Strategies for Qualitative Research*. Chicago: Aldine, 1967.

Glass, Gene V. "Primary, secondary, and meta analysis of research." *Educational Researcher* 5, no. 11 (1976):3–8.

Glass, Gene V. "Policy for the Unpredictable (Uncertainty Research and Policy)." *Educational Researcher* 8, no. 9 (1979):12–14.

Griliches, Zvi; Hall, B. H.; and Hausman, Jerome A. "Missing Data and Self-Selection in Large Panels." *Annales de l'INSEE*, nos. 30–31 (1978).

Heckman, James J. "The Common Structure of Statistical Models of Truncation, Sample Selection and Limited Dependent Variables and a Simple Estimator for Such Models." *Annals of Economic and Social Measurement* 5 (1976):475–92.

Heckman, James J. "Sample Selection Bias as a Specification Error." *Econometrica* 47 (1979):153–61.

Keen, Peter G. W., and Morton, M. S. Scott. *Decision Support*

Systems: An Organizational Perspective. Reading, Mass.: Addison-Wesley Publishing Co., 1978.

Kuhn, Thomas S. *The Essential Tension: Selected Studies in Scientific Tradition and Change.* Chicago: University of Chicago Press, 1978.

Lawley, D. "A Note on Karl Pearson's Selection Formula." *Royal Society of Edinburgh, Proceedings, Section A*, 62 (1943–44):28–30.

Levitan, S. K., and Wurzburg, Gregory. *Evaluating Federal Social Programs: An Uncertain Art.* Kalamazoo, Mich.: W. E. Upjohn Institute, 1979.

Lindblom, Charles E. *The Intelligence of Democracy: Decision-making through Mutual Adjustment.* New York: Free Press, 1965.

Lindblom, Charles E., and Cohen, David K. *Usable Knowledge: Social Science and Social Problem Solving.* New Haven, Conn.: Yale University Press, 1979.

Linn, Robert L. "Single-Group Validity, Differential Validity, and Differential Prediction." *Journal of Applied Psychology* 63 (1978):507–12.

Linn, Robert L., and Werts, C. E. "Considerations for Studies of Test Bias." *Journal of Educational Measurement* 8 (1971):1–4.

Lynd, Robert S. *Knowledge for What? The Place of Social Science in American Culture.* Princeton, N.J.: Princeton University Press, 1939.

Lyons, Gene M. *The Uneasy Partnership.* New York: Russell Sage Foundation, 1969.

McGuire, William J. "The Yin and Yang of Progress in Social Psychology: Seven Koan." *Journal of Personality and Social Psychology* 28 (1973):446–56.

MacKenzie, Brian D. *Behaviorism and the Limits of Scientific Method.* Atlantic Highlands, N.J.: Humanities Press, 1977.

Mackie, John L. *The Cement of the Universe: A Study of Causation.* Oxford: Clarendon Press, 1974.

Maddala, G. S. "Self-Selectivity Problems in Econometric Models." In P. R. Krishnaiah (ed.), *Applications of Statistics.* Amsterdam: North-Holland, 1977.

Meehl, Paul E. "Theory-Testing in Psychology and Physics: A Methodological Paradox." *Philosophy of Science* 34 (1967):103–15.

Meehl, Paul E. "Nuisance Variables and the *ex-post facto* Design." In M. Radner and S. Winokur (eds.), *Minnesota Studies in the Philosophy of Science*. Vol. 4. Minneapolis: University of Minnesota Press, 1970.

Meehl, Paul E. "High School Yearbooks: A Reply to Schwartz." *Journal of Abnormal Psychology* 77 (1971):143–48.

Meehl, Paul E. "Theoretical Risks and Tabular Asterisks: Sir Karl, Sir Ronald, and the Slow Progress of Soft Psychology." *Journal of Consulting and Clinical Psychology* 46 (1978): 806–34.

Myrdal, Gunnar. "How Scientific Are the Social Sciences?" *Journal of Social Issues* 28, no. 4 (1973).

Nelson, Richard R. *The Moon and the Ghetto*. New York: W. W. Norton & Co., 1977.

Pillemer, D. E., and Light, R. J. "Using the Results of Randomized Experiments to Construct Social Programs: Three Caveats." In L. Sechrest and others (eds.), *Evaluation Studies Review Annual*. Vol. 4. Beverly Hills, Calif.: Sage Publications, 1979.

Popper, Karl R. *The Poverty of Historicism*. 3d ed. London: Routledge & Kegan Paul, 1961.

Prewitt, Kenneth. "Testimony before the Subcommittee on Science, Research, and Technology, House of Representatives." *Items* 34, no. 1 (March 1980):1–4.

Rasch, Gunnar. "On General Laws and the Meaning of Measurement in Psychology." In J. Neyman (ed.), *Proceedings, Fourth Berkeley Symposium on Mathematical Statistics and Probability*. Vol. 4. Berkeley: University of California Press, 1961.

Rein, Martin. *Social Science and Public Policy*. New York: Penguin Books, 1976.

Rescher, Nicholas. *Scientific Explanation*. New York: Free Press, 1970.

Rivlin, Alice M. *Systematic Thinking for Social Action*. Washington, D.C.: Brookings Institution, 1971.

Rivlin, Alice M. "Allocating Resources for Policy Research: How Can Experiments Be More Useful?" *American Economic Association, Addresses and Proceedings* 64 (1974):346–54.

Rossi, Peter H. "Past, Present, and Future Prospects of Evaluation Research." In L.-E. Datta and R. Perloff (eds.), *Improving Evaluations*. Beverly Hills, Calif.: Sage Publications, 1979.

Sanford, R. N. "Whatever Happened to Action Research?" *Journal of Social Issues* 26, no. 4 (1970):3–23.

Schmidt, Frank L.; Berner, J. G.; and Hunter, John E. "Racial Differences in Validity of Employment Tests: Reality or Illusion?" *Journal of Applied Psychology* 58 (1973):5–9.

Schmidt, Frank L.; Hunter, John E.; McKenzie, Robert C.; and Muldrow, Tressie W. "Impact of Valid Selection Procedures on Work-Force Productivity." *Journal of Applied Psychology* 64 (1979):609–26.

Schultze, Charles. *The Politics and Economics of Public Spending.* Washington, D.C.: Brookings Institution, 1968.

Schutz, Richard E. "Where We've Been, Where We Are, and Where We're Going in Educational R & D." *Educational Researcher* 8, no. 8 (1979):6–8, 24.

Simon, Herbert A. *The Sciences of the Artificial.* Cambridge, Mass.: M.I.T. Press, 1969.

Simon, Herbert A. "From Substantive to Procedural Rationality." In S. J. Latsis (ed.), *Method and Appraisal in Economics.* Cambridge: Cambridge University Press, 1976.

Small, Albion W. *The Meaning of Social Science.* Chicago: University of Chicago Press, 1910.

Webb, Noreen. "Learning in Individual and Small Group Settings." Ph.D. dissertation, Stanford University, 1978.

Weiss, Carol H. (ed.). *Using Social Research in Public Policy Making.* Lexington, Mass.: D. C. Heath & Co. 1977.

Wicker, Allen W. "Ecological Psychology: Some Recent and Prospective Developments." *American Psychologist* 34 (1979):755–65.

Wilensky, Harold. *Organizational Intelligence: Knowledge and Policy in Government and Industry.* New York: Basic Books, 1967.

6

Response to Lecture by Professor Cronbach

Philip E. Converse

UNIVERSITY OF MICHIGAN

First let me thank you all for the chance to engage in the fiftieth anniversary proceedings. I found them very provocative, as the remainder of this letter may suggest. I was particularly intrigued by your Monday night comments about a certain downbeat atmosphere in general. I had hoped that Tuesday might allow time for more of a discussion of that fact, but the clock was relentless.

I thought I might chip in here with a few reactions for your private amusement, since I still have it on my mind. Actually, although I no longer remember the particulars, I had sensed a rather surprising downbeat tone even before we went over to Breasted Hall on Sunday, and had begun wondering about it. By evening, and with Hanna Gray's extended quotations from 1954, I began to realize what was going on. It seemed clearly an expectations problem, since to my way of thinking the 1954 expectations were out of sight, and we obviously were not in 1979 where they thought we'd be.

If that is the downbeat, then I am not much worried about it, since I missed out on those 1954 expectations and have never much shared them. I am a fifth of a generation or more behind many of the speakers, and actually started my first formal training in social science in 1954. I can vaguely remember that type of euphoria when I started, but I did not take it very seriously.

As a matter of fact, a very major formative experience for me in these regards was an evening in 1959 in a little town in the southwest of France when I encountered Duncan MacRae and we spent the evening talking globally about social science. He was despondent about the state of these disciplines, and after some grilling what it really seemed to come down to was that social scientists had been gunning away for forty years, or seventy years, or one hundred (depending on whom you count), and we hadn't even had Newton yet. The Newton part, incidentally, was very explicit in Duncan's thought. We had a spirited debate, because I was so thunderstruck at why anybody would have expected a Newton performance at that stage in social science development. Even if one took a physical science "clock" parallel in the most mechanical way, it seemed to me quite premature.

But more to the point, there are to me manifest differences in the textures of different subject matters, and it seemed to me that the raw materials of social science—any of them—are much more complex in their structure than the things Newton had to work with. I felt that would slow down the social science clock enormously. And finally, more important yet, I wasn't even certain that there might ever be a culmination in social science like the Newton one, at least in pure form, or that we would wither on the vine without it.

In any event, this conversation made a deep impression on me, because I came to see that there were other expectation structures than my own plodding century-by-century view. Sunday night I began to think perhaps it was no coincidence that Duncan MacRae was at the time with you at Chicago, and had probably blown in from Berkeley sometime near the 1954 celebration.

About then I labeled a drawer in my cognitive files "Waiting for Newton," and have been collecting bits and pieces in it ever since. At one point or another I had added the phrase "like waiting for Godot" to it, saving it all for just the right occasion; and was amused when Lee Cronbach beat me to it in his talk.

He even used it as I would have, as a label for remarkably unrealistic expectations. Moreover, I have very little disagreement with most of the facts cited in Lee's talk, although I do quarrel with what we make of it. It seemed to me that Lee is remarkably depressed by the discovery that basic relationships can be found to undergo some remarkable sea changes across time and across cultures. On the other hand, there is an amazing leap from the citation of a few such instances to the conclusion that no general laws exist.

I have done a lot of cross-cultural work, and could add greatly to the list of things that change surprisingly across time or culture. On the other hand, I also have a long list of things that have been remarkably constant, or near-constant, over the same spans. I wouldn't count on any one of these, and perhaps not on any of them, always to be observable in just the same way, not matter where or when. On the other hand, I am very far from imagining that some extremely general accounts cannot be wrought that would be quite powerful; and, with a little luck, one might even get up a further notch in generality and even be able to subsume the rare exceptions. On the inductive side, at least, one place you start is precisely to begin to see what entities flop around on you in time and space, and which one's don't, in order to see where you can most profitably put your theoretic weight. There are often surprises in this sorting, but they run both ways, and the surprises are after all what inquiry is about.

It seems to me more generally that if there are a lot of Flat Earth people about, and I agree there are (they are in my Waiting for Newton file too), it is shortcomings in social science instruction that have created them. I don't much rue a Flat Earth generation, because it is not tactically unreasonable as a first cut at a subject matter to see how far you can get being simple and linear-additive and all that. I think that tactic actually has carried us farther than Lee does. But there is a difference between implying that if it doesn't work we may as well get discouraged and quit; or moving on to more complex models.

The disservice that much of our training has done is to create a very poorly balanced picture of even what the "hard" sciences look like. For most of our students, science is Newton and Einstein, period, or with a step greater sophistication you add Maxwell and quantum mechanics. These are roughly the final day's climb up Everest from the last base camp, and the endless scrabbling around in the foothills that got you to the last base camp is not conveyed at all.

Moreover, I don't think that it is merely a timing and staging matter. Sure the Everests are there, and sooner or later it would be nice to get up to where you can make the last assault. It is also extremely helpful to have them on the horizon as ideals so that you can maintain a sort of persistent upward direction.

But the fact of the matter is that hard science is absolutely littered with very serviceable and illuminating theories with textures different from $E = mc^2$. There are in fact whole compartments full of theories messy in texture (relative to Newton) which are not messy simply because they temporally lack the closure that some Newton will shortly give them, but which nobody would ever expect (given the aims and the texture of the raw materials) to culminate in such a mountaintop, yet which are enormously valuable contributions to human culture.

In many of these cases, such as the study of turbulence, the raw materials look much more like our own than what Newton had to work with. Another currently exciting development of a messy theory is the theory of plate tectonics. Now you can define theory in such a way as to say that is not a theory at all, because it does not now, nor will it ever, have the Newton or Einstein texture. (I know full well that here and there work on plate tectonics is speeded up because investigators can reach in their back pockets for certain pieces of precise knowledge that is around because of theory of the Newton-Einstein type, and because of many other wads of much messier theory they have back there. We do not have too much in our back pockets to help our work on messy theories, although I would deny that we have none, and I expect we will have increasing amounts as time wears on. The important point is that plate tectonics is realistically not even headed in a Newton-Einstein direction.) I am less patient with purists saying that such cerebration is not "theory" than I am with any claim that such is not science or not illuminating and abundantly useful to know about.

(I personally have found it illuminating because as a child I had a world map in my bedroom and was crushed when I was told with Ultimate Authority that of course Africa and South America never split off from one another. It is also a productive theory because it has produced the political slogan, to be splashed in black spray paint, "Reunite Gondwanaland!!!")

Seriously, though, science is filled with such messy theories. I often think that a good half of our social sciences—the more "historicist" macrohalf—would be much better off looking to geology for models of messy theories than to physics. But we don't teach those: science is physics and does not even embrace the large demimonde of *that* discipline.

Moreover, I don't even know where it is written that good and useful social science theories two hundred years from now will have to have the texture of any yet seen in other sciences. New textures emerge like new theories: "game theory" is, for example, a very odd fish in these terms. It most closely resembles a mathematical theory but is a bit off-color for that. This is in part because it has real-world yearnings, although these don't realistically carry very far without piling on a lot of further assumptions. Should we throw it out because it is hard to tell what kind of a theory it really is? I think not.

Science is even populated—if not littered—with messy variables that social scientists know nothing about, but should. Although I haven't tried it out in a group as august as we had assembled over the weekend, I have yet to find a common working social scientist who has ever heard of what are callled "dimensionless numbers" in physical science, much less appreciates that at points they have been very useful. As a matter of fact, most are horrified at my description of what a dimensionless number is, because from their training they know at once that such an entity has to be a no-no if we are going to do "real" science.

My favorite starter is the cartoon showing a highway winding into a small town, with a big sign in the foreground which says:

Entering Jeffersonville
Population: 500
Altitude: 430 ft.
Latitude: <u>40° N.</u>
Total   970

The 970 is an example of what scientists call a dimensionless number—perhaps a misnomer, and certainly frivolous in this case. But the fact of the matter is that there are a variety of such numbers lying around in physical science that turn out to be tremendously useful tools. A Rayleigh number, for example, is a weird concoction which requires that you add together three or four utterly incommensurate quanta, such as (I don't remember actual details) pressure expressed in pounds per square inch, temperature in degrees Celsius, specific gravity of the medium expressed in something else. When the Rayleigh number passes some threshold like 1,268, say, then reliably there is a sudden sea change in the nature of the phenomena you witness, the weights of governing parameters or even what the governing parameters are, etc., etc.—a whole new ball game. As I recall, another new ball game arises when the Rayleigh number gets out near 2,000.

This is a piece of fluid dynamics, I believe—there are other such numbers in optics and elsewhere. They are not usually mere inductive accidents, and the Rayleigh numbers fell out of equations Lord Rayleigh was working on which had some prior theoretical pedigree. Nonetheless, it is not hard to imagine that entities like dimensionless numbers might come to be highly useful in empirical work on, say, revolution, a hundred or two years down the road. But then, any good social scientist knows that such work is not scientific, because it has nothing to do with Everest out there and is dirty and messy to boot. On to Everest instead.

Well, I didn't intend to maunder on at this length, and the point should be obvious. It is we who have reared a generation with Flat Earth and Newton expectations, and the fact that neither our world nor for that matter even "real" science looks much like that should not produce despair.

I was amused some years ago when I saw in an editorial by a distinguished biologist that all biologists are aware that they suffer a unique affliction in that discipline. In biology, he said (believe me, this was straight face), it seems that every question answered merely kicks up ten new ones. A pity, I thought, that those biologists can't get anything off the ground, or even permanently and immutably settled like we or the particle physicists have.

I heard that line, predictably, in the Anniversary celebration, and I think it was said even more than once. It was colored negative, and this makes sense because who wants to spend a lot of time answering four questions and finding that by then you are forty questions deeper in debt? But you can also color it positive and clap hands and sing. It is, after all, the progress of inquiry.

Perhaps I am just an incurable optimist. But while my expectations and sights seem different than those of the 1954 galaxy, I don't think that I am counseling us to ignore self-searching questions as to the progress we are making and ways we might jiggle the inquiry system to step up the pace. I worry loads about that, in fact. But I never assume I have reason to know just how long the ultimate tunnel is—I even doubt that is an appropriate metaphor, given the preceding paragraphs. My morale depends on whether I can see signs that we are in fact inching along, and I demand such evidence, from year to year. Herb Simon had a little passage in his remarks, a bit before the coda, which said in effect, look: we are making serious progress, and here are some examples. His list could be amply added to, all over the social science map. These are the kinds of bearings I keep my eye out for, also.

I had intended to devote the second half of this letter to a set of comments stimulated by the symposium regarding 1954 expectations about the role of social science research in the formation of public policy. As I am running far too long, let me limit myself to one extended comment about a dilemma commonly encountered at that interface.

The specific dilemma I want to address involves the gross misfit between the short time frames within which policymakers typically operate and the longer time frames necessary for worthwhile social science research. This is certainly not the only serious dilemma encountered at the research/policy interface, and Lee Cronbach, Herb Simon, and others commented wisely on a much longer list, some still more basic. Nonetheless, I would suppose that in any ranking of such dilemma, the time frame problem would fall in the top five.

In an implicit way, I was talking about problems of this type in my own remarks, since I referred to instances in which hastily drawn and hastily evaluated public opinion data did arrive rapidly enough to have some bearing on the current stream of policy formation, although with less than helpful outcomes because of the haste involved. Some policy problems requiring decisions linger long enough in a particular form that careful research can be completed. More often, however, it seems that when policy demands touch off the mounting of some elaborate social science research, the results only come through after the policy makers have either been forced to stop-gap decisions, or have redefined the problem because of the flow of events, or have their attention swept four or five problems farther down the road, so that whatever the results, they don't much care any more. This is naturally frustrating on both sides.

This dilemma is deep and intrinsic. I have no neat solutions, but perhaps there are more useful ways of coping with the dilemma than often seem to be employed.

Some things said in the symposium carried me back to a day in the latter stages of the Vietnam War, when I happened to be sitting with a colleague at the point when the media first broke the news that the United States was embarked on a program of strategic bombing in Southeast Asia. He groaned in despair and said in effect, "My god, don't tell me we have to learn that lesson all over again."

Although not one of the principal investigators, this colleague had had close familiarity with the large-scale assessment of the strategic bombing carried out by the United States near the end of World War II and had participated in the designing of the survey research involved. The full assessment of that strategic bombing program spread across an intricate array of impact questions, including effects on traffic patterns and a myriad of other relatively technical or operations research questions. His involvement was with the segment of the assessment where social science research was most central: the impact of the bombing on civilian morale.

The questions to be answered by the research was not whether strategic bombing would actually produce an erosion of civilian morale. It was obvious on commonsense grounds that it would have such an effect. The real questions were instead ones of optimization, such as the circumstances under which civilian morale would collapse farthest and fastest, as bombing investments varied.

Three particulars of this strategic bombing assessment are worth our attention. The first is the ultimate result. The researchers were unable to specify the circumstances under which civilian morale collapsed most readily, because the research suggested that civilian morale did not collapse at all. In fact, some concluded that the strategic bombing was actually counterproductive, although this reading may have gone beyond the data. However this may be, the result was sharply counterintuitive, and in view of frequent charges that social science research mainly elaborates what anyone would know in advance, had a certain charm.

The second particular involves the scope of the effort, which involved large-scale survey research in both West Germany and Japan. The amount of money actually invested is unknown, but, given the level and numbers of research personnel involved, the distances traversed and the difficulties of erecting suitable sampling frames on an ad hoc basis in countries just ravaged by war, it seems very likely that the civilian morale segment of the strategic bombing assessment taken by itself represented one of the largest investments in social research ever witnessed up to its time.

The final particular brings us back to the matter of time frames. Why was such a large investment made when the likelihood of results affecting current policy was low? Actually, the research teams were in the edges of occupied Germany before V-E Day, and it is at least conceivable that some decisionmaker fancied that the feedback of results might yet affect military strategy in the successful termination of the war, especially in the Pacific theater. As is so often the case, these latter social science results arrived too late to be of immediate policy use. On the other hand, the continuation of the research suggests that some policymakers felt the results would be of use, if not now, then "next time."

In short, then, we have a major counterintuitive result, purchased very dearly, on grounds that while too tardy to be of current use it would be worth knowing for "next time."

I could complete my irony in a trice if I might say that all this work had been forgotten in formulating the policy decisions to launch a program of strategic bombing in Southeast Asia a quarter century later. I cannot say this, for I have no idea what went into that decision, nor would I have much chance of finding out. It is certainly true that sapping of civilian morale is not the only reason for such a program. Conceivably, the relevant decisionmakers were highly mindful of the civilian morale results from the World War II assessment but went ahead on other grounds; or perhaps they felt that results achieved for the populations of industrialized states like Germany and Japan could not be generalized to the underdeveloped areas in Asia.

Nonetheless, in stray reading in the intervening period, I have more than once encountered references by observers close to the strategic bombing program in Southeast Asia, who seem to imply that a very major purpose of the program was to gut the resistance of the civilian populations involved, and who express surprise and chagrin at the fact that subsequent evidence indicates that the bombings achieved no detectible erosion of civilian morale, and may even have stiffened popular resistance.

By now it should be clear where I am headed: if there is an insoluble discrepancy between the time frame available to the policymaker to make peace with a first problem in order to get to the next before it gets out of hand, and the time frame necessary for social science to generate respectable results about the first problem, then perhaps we should worry less about the frustrations of always being late and hence irrelevant, and more about how to make research on the "this-time" problem more useful for evaluation when the "next-time" occurs, as it almost invariably will.

It should also be clear, by the way, what in the symposium produced my particular train of thought, since Lee Cronbach touched base with the strategic bombing problem in his remarks. His context was different. In fact, his context runs utterly cross-grain to mine, since I am suggesting that we should not ignore yesterday's research in tackling today's problems, and his point was that the British were stung in World War II by assuming too glibly that lessons derived from the putting down of a tribal insurrection in Iraq in the 1920s through saturation bombing could be profitably transported across time and cultures as a prescription for strategic bombing in Germany in World War II, when in point of fact the very same evidence I have reviewed suggests that in the German case this "treatment" was at best nonproductive and perhaps even counterproductive. As he notes, by way of underscoring the imprudent generalization of findings, "The Reich was not a tribal village."

To which the obvious response is, "Neither were the tribal villages of Southeast Asia the Reich," even though the dominant impression seems to be that under the impact of strategic bombing the population responded in the same way as German civilians a quarter of a century before. This leaves the British Iraqi experience as something of an odd man out, although it does not strike me as painfully odd. After all, there was a massive program of strategic bombing in both Germany and Japan aimed at corroding civilian morale, and both Germans and Japanese soon thereafter surrendered. I gather this is exactly what happened in Iraq as well. In the World War II case, there was some rather elaborate intervening research to shoot down the assumption that strategic bombing had gutted civilian morale and hence had produced a surrender. I rather doubt that there was any corresponding research in the Iraqi case. In other words, perhaps what seems to be a gross discrepancy in human response has less to do with the frailties of generalizing across twenty years of history, a quarter of the globe, and goodness knows how much distance in social

and economic structure than it does with the discrepancy between a major research effort and none to speak of.

I raise these points with some trepidation, because I could
not agree more with Cronbach that there are several perils in
generalizing many social science "findings" across time and
space. I have seen these perils many times, and close at hand, so
I do not care to be coded among the glib. I am not claiming that
since the surveys of civilian morale in the 1940s and impressions
gleaned from Southeast Asia around 1970 seem to show about the
same thing, that there is no point in expecting anything else
wherever, whenever, and whatever the circumstances. The
things at stake are hardly "laws."

On the other hand, I feel devoutly that evidence of this kind
ought at the very least to budge our a priori distributions of felt
probabilities (in the Bayesian sense) about outcomes in some
significant degree, the vagaries of transport in time and space
notwithstanding. That is, the Air Force in 1944 clearly felt that the
odds were 98–2 or 99–1 that strategic bombing would make at
least some inroads on civilian morale. Thirty years later, the degree of surprise registered at the apparent lack of inroads made by
strategic bombing in Southeast Asia suggests to me observers
whose expectations were still lopsided to the tune of 95–5 or
more, despite intervening research that said the contrary.

This appalls me, especially as the research was costly and dedicated to "next time." I suspect Lee Cronbach would agree with
my distress. If he is saying that, due to potential variability in
culture and time, not to mention fragilities in the research process
itself, we should not approach further strategic decisions with a
prioris shifted all the way back to 0–100 on the basis of the World
War II assays, I would heartily agree as well. At this point I might
want 30–70, or 40–60, and he might more cautiously choose
60–40. But these differences are now reduced to nuances, and my
primary point is the modest one that the intervention of some
serious research on the topic has and should have made a difference in our expectations about the world.

Fred Mosteller (1980) has noted that new ideas springing from
evaluative research take a long time to "seep through," and that
perhaps we should have expectations of a twenty-five-year lag
rather than any instantaneous "take." This observation fits with
the call for more realistic expectations about social science gen-

erally, with which I began this letter. At the same time, I wonder if a more frank recognition in advance that a "next time" use is about the best one could hope for might not affect the design of such research in helpful ways. Among other things, for example, it might induce some minimization of highly topical and phenotypic elements in the assessment, relative to what is likely to be more generic in the problem under scrutiny. In other words, it might yield assessments shifted at least a few notches farther along that long continuum that lies between "purely" applied and "purely" basic research.

I'm sure this is enough for one response. Let me say again that it was a lovely and stimulating visit. I came away not even discouraged.

REFERENCE

Mosteller, Frederick. "Acceptance of the Lazarsfeld Prize." In Clark C. Abt (ed.), *Problems in American Social Policy Research*. Cambridge, Mass.: Abt Books, 1980.

7 Policy, Research, and Political Theory

James S. Coleman
UNIVERSITY OF CHICAGO

The University convocation takes place four times a year. These are important points for reflection and self-examination. In June, greatest attention is properly paid to undergraduates receiving their first university degree. In August, it is appropriate to focus upon the new Ph.D.s who are eager to get their degrees before reporting to their first teaching jobs in September. In March and December, it is useful to address some of the other activities of which the university is composed. I shall do that today. But I do it not primarily as a matter of interest for those of us now occupying the university as its faculty, but for those of you who, receiving your degrees now, will be occupying it in the future. It is to you, then, that my comments about policy, research, and political theory are directed.

Within the last fifteen years a new phenomenon has arisen in the social sciences in the United States—though properly speaking, it cannot be said to be *in* the social sciences. The phenomenon is a kind of research that may be generically termed "social policy research." It has included *social experiments* such as income maintenance experiments, housing allowance experiments, and health insurance experiments, and *evaluations*, such as the hotly debated evaluations of Head Start, and including evaluations of hundreds of other programs in education, in community mental health centers, in welfare reform, in employment training programs, and other areas of social policy.

Some of this social policy research has been carried out at universities. Some has been carried out at independent research organizations which have sprung up and grown in the 1970s much as did the physical research laboratories like Argonne in the 1940s

Presented as the 375th Convocation Address, University of Chicago, December 18, 1979. Originally published in the *University of Chicago Record* 14, no. 2 (April 4, 1980):78–80.

and 1950s. Some of these research organizations are large and relatively stable. Others, which have grown like mushrooms around Washington, are small, and many have short lifetimes. Until this new "social policy research," a common complaint of social scientists was that policy makers never paid attention to research; it was never used. This complaint is still heard, but it is more muted now. For much of this recent research has been extensively used. The evaluations that found little effect of Head Start probably prevented massive expansions of the program, though they did not overcome the momentum of the existing program. The income maintenance experiments which showed the great impact of income maintenance programs in increasing divorce and inhibiting remarriage were partly responsible for killing the recent negative income tax proposals in Congress. The evaluations showing strong educational benefits of Sesame Street gave impetus to the growth of that program and its descendants. The examples could be continued at length.

So the question is no longer: "Why is social research not being used in social policy?" It is, rather, a more serious question: "Is the extent and nature of its use beneficial to society or harmful?" So long as the research that social scientists engage in is irrelevant to the functioning of society, they can be safely left to play in their sandbox. But when it begins to be *used*, it is necessary to examine a little more closely what is going on.

The question of whether social policy research is beneficial or harmful cannot yet be answered; it is still too soon. The answer is *not*, however, the simple one; it is not merely a question of whether the research is well done and technically correct. Let us assume that to be the case, and ask the question again: Assuming that social policy research gives correct answers to the questions posed for it: Is its introduction into policy-making a good thing or a bad thing? The answer to this question depends largely on what effect it has on the distribution of power in society.

To begin an answer, it is useful to turn to a thread of neo-Marxist political philosophy that has become strong in Germany, and has particularly found voice in the sociologist Jurgen Habermas. Habermas envisions a "rational society" as a pre-eminent danger of the future: a society with a feedback process from policy effects back to policy makers, bypassing the political process and emasculating the class interests generated by the institutional structure of society. The vision is of societies in which there is "the end of ideology," to use Daniel Bell's imagery, governed by nonpolitical technocrats informed by sophisticated feedback mechanisms.

And the feedback mechanism, of course, is this recent arrival on the political scene, social policy research. Thus in the vision of the future, social policy research undermines the normal political processes by giving the technocratic policy makers that most important weapon: information.

This suggests that social policy research aids the centralization of power, helping to create a monolithic authority system. But observation of cases of such research suggets that matters may be somewhat different. A number of examples suggest that social policy research is more useful to outsiders than to insiders, more useful to the potential opponents of policy than to the policy makers themselves.

In my experience, this observation holds with surprising regularity: research on effects of Head Start was most helpful to opponents of Head Start, because it found few effects; the income maintenance experiments were most helpful to opponents of the proposed policy, because they *did* find effects; research in effects of school desegregation has been used by plaintiffs in court cases to oppose student assignment policies in local school districts, and so on. The generalization does not hold in every case, but does in many.

Why? I believe the most fundamental reason is that research results, when they show defects of policy, legitimate opposition to the policy. Policy makers have already the legitimation provided by political and have little need for additional legitimation. But opponents, lacking the power of political authority, gain the legitimacy of "scientific truth" or "scientific evidence," which can constitute an important weapon in the political struggle.

Why this contradiction between the neo-Marxist vision of the "rational society" and the generalization I have just remarked upon? One source, I think, is the failure of Habermas and others to recognize the powerful legitimation that scientific evidence provides for alternative values. Its potential role in subverting political authority is similar to that which religion has always provided, as a competing way of defining what is "right."

Another source of the difference, however, is an implicit

assumption of Habermas that is met in some social policy research, but not all: an assumption that the feedback process is one in which the research questions are posed by the policy maker and the research results are privately transmitted back to the policy maker. In the examples I cited earlier where policy research is more useful to outsiders than insiders, the research results were openly published, and the design was broad enough to address a variety of interests.

Social policy research in the United States hovers near the borderline of meeting the assumption of private communication between researcher and policy maker. One can see the proximity of the borderline through examples. The result on divorce which affected the negative income tax proposals was first found in 1974 by sociologists at Stanford University. The results were first denied by the experiment's designers in the Department of Health, Education and Welfare, then bottled up, then obscured, until they finally came into the open for policy deliberation in Congressional hearings in 1978. There are numerous other such examples, despite the existence of some laws and some procedures which facilitate the pluralistic use of policy research.

What can be said, I think, is that social policy research *can* come to have an effect on public policy in the direction of undercutting pluralism, or it can come to have an effect in strengthening pluralism, depending wholly on how it is institutionalized. The examples I've given indicate some of the elements that should be taken into consideration if pluralism is to be strengthened. More generally, however, this is a matter for political theory. The political theorists and practitioners who designed the American Constitution were very attentive to insuring pluralism in political decision-making: separate branches of government to provide checks and balances, and a bicameral legislature. But the society they dealt with was small, comprehensible, and not one in which information about its functioning was a scarce good. As a consequence, their political theory had no place for pluralism in the systematic provision of information about societal functioning. There was the freedom of speech amendment which helped insure a free press, but otherwise little. Into this vacuum came, from early days, certain institutions, especially Congressional hearings, and agency hearings in the executive branch. Along with these institutions came the extensive structure of interest group representation which above all provides information—certainly not unbiased information, but information nevertheless.

Now, however, with the explosive growth of social policy research, which can constitute a private instrument, privately used, for government agencies, or a public instrument, publicly available for pluralistic use by any and all, an augmentation of political theory is necessary. In its absence, the danger is that he who pays the piper calls the tune, and that social policy research becomes a private instrument of government agencies, undercutting the structure of interest-based political pluralism in the society.

What is the university's role in this? It is to provide the autonomous base for social policy research. Nearly all the examples I know in which policy research has arrived at results that throw doubt on federal policies and has insisted that the results be publicly available, are cases in which the analyst was *not* in a contract research organization wholly dependent on government funds, but was a university faculty member.

And the university's role as well is to provide the context within which a political theory of information pluralism comes to be developed. For such a theory, followed by institutional safeguards, will help insure that the vision of a "rational society of the future," governed as a monolithic authority system, will not be realized.

And it is not we, who are at the university now, but those of you who are leaving it, who are receiving your degrees now and will be occupying universities in the next generation, to whom this task will fall. I commend it to your attention, and I am confident you will be equal to the task.

8 The Citizen and the Scholar: Ships That Crash in the Night

Barry D. Karl

UNIVERSITY OF CHICAGO

Scholarship is not a profitable occupation in the simple economic sense in which we understand profitability. It shares with art and pure science a need for support, which makes its practitioners dependent on the willingness of donors to support activities the primary and immediate benefit of which will be some form of gratification other than wealth. In the long run, it is argued, donors or their heirs will benefit. The culture will be improved, the future of civilizations enriched; but the bottom line, as we are fond of saying today, is no different in the short run than it has ever been. Regardless of the nature of the state and its economic structure, scholars and scholarship require the patronage of whatever source of wealth there is in the community, whether it be private individuals or the public treasury; and that patronage must rest on a sense of gift which acknowledges a limited and distant utility as more important than a standard return on investment.

There are additional factors, too, that make support of scholarship questionable as a traditionally profitable investment. Scholarship is not an identifiable commodity with a predictable performance, and scholars have a record of raising questions that may unsettle the world around them. Scholars are members of the communities which support them, and they are by no means agreed on their relation to their communities. Dependent though they may be by the very nature of their occupation and the general definition of its economic worth, they nonetheless claim an independence which they see as the essential requirement of eminence even among themselves. Patronage is an uneasy state of being for everyone concerned.

The American use of the term "patronage" has always had a slightly un-American cast to it, but from two quite different perspectives. The term has referred, for the most part, either to the

101

distribution of political jobs or to support for the arts, a pair of extremes not customarily linked—low corruption and high culture. For generations of American reformers political patronage has stood for the circumventing of democratic choice at best, dishonesty and favoritism at worst. Support for the arts, too, has always carried with it a sense of elitist culture building that distinguished Art with a capital A from popular entertainment.

I should like to draw on an older usage common to a period of history when the two extremes were not so extreme, or were connected along a continuum that assumed everyone who engaged in intellectual pursuits either depended upon inherited wealth or on the willingness of some individual or some institution with money to support them. Much of what we consider culture in Western Civilization was funded essentially by wealth accumulated by various royal aristocracies or religious groups. The assumption that the eighteenth-century democratic revolutions would produce a culture different from the courtly culture of the fallen monarchies or the religious culture of the Church was a central belief among those who troubled over the issue of intellectual life in a democratic society. The idea that the arts and sciences would simply shift their funding base from the royal treasury to the public trough was not initially the dominant point of view among those who believed that the new democracies required arts and sciences appropriate to their needs. While in Europe, generally speaking, the shift from aristocratic to public funding did take place in one form or another, Americans resisted such a transfer. One has only to note how recent is the development of federal patronage for intellectual life in the United States to puzzle over the question of the American view of such funding and its relation to cultural development. The traditional association with wartime emergencies, international political interests, domestic economic and social crisis, or populist politics of one kind or another has always been strong. The emphasis upon practicality and popular will continues to limit the ability of government at all levels to provide sustained support for endeavors which can be subjected to public criticism.

The private system of patronage which developed in the United States at the turn of the century was itself a peculiar phenomenon. In the decades after the Civil War Ohio grain and whiskey merchants of relatively modest means invested in western oil and railroads, amassing in the process wealth so enormous that its continued accumulation and reinvestment became a threat to economic stability. For whatever their complex of reasons, the decisions the millionaires made to give away large parts of their fortunes resulted in the establishment of a private system of patronage one would have to return to the Renaissance to duplicate. Many of them, of course, did precisely that when they built and furnished their homes on upper Fifth Avenue.

From the turn of the century until the Second World War, a period when no legislator who valued reelection would openly support research not immediately definable as practical, and certainly nothing that could be considered "artistic," middle-class American monarchs created by the nation's post–Civil War industrial expansion did it for them. All of these matters involve a history of patronage we are only beginning to trace. Some of these tracings reveal directions that were clear enough long before the recent availability of archival materials made it possible for historians to footnote their suspicions. John D. Rockefeller and Andrew Carnegie, for example, believed in Capitalism and felt that their benefactions would support its continued existence, if not its world wide expansion in what they considered its special American form. Although the distinction may seem too subtle, it does make a difference whether one says "would support" or "should support," for it seems clear that as they examined their own lives they came to the conclusion that American Capitalism was based on a mystical history that had emerged out of a world history Tocqueville had described many years earlier. That history, they believed, would be supported by research unless that research were inhibited by foreign revolutionary impulses or internal subversive pressures. Research would not impose beliefs but would liberate beliefs inherently a part of the universal human condition. One has to guard against the temptation to credit them with more sophisticated intellects and powers of ideological control and international manipulation.

While such points are presently beginning to undergo historiographic debate, there is a side of the problem which is possibly in danger of being neglected. Instead of asking, "Why did they give the way they gave?" we might ask, "Why did our historical counterparts in the academic community accept what they had to give?" It's a question that raises some issues that were being debated throughout the period, and they were issues filled with some rather remarkable complexities. They may help explain the way the very concept of patronage was transformed, or perhaps it would be better to say "buried." By resurrecting it, if only briefly, we may be able to ask some different and rather interesting questions.

Let us discard the most obvious answer first, that they accepted because they had to eat. It's too true to be very useful; but it doesn't explain either the energy or the enthusiasm with which they gorged themselves. Nor does it explain their inability to fashion alternatives or to work out the implications of the alternatives they were able to consider. The fact that they did have alternatives and that they did consider them is itself a vaguely concealed aspect of the period couched more often in curmudgeonly critical attacks than in programmatic debates.

In accepting their patronage, we can ask, How did the community of scholars define its relation to its patrons and its responsibilities to its sources of support? Again, if we start with the supposition that private funding was a precursor of government funding which has, in the last decade, overtaken the private resources, are we asking any larger philosophical questions about the relation between the scholar and the state?

Let me start by pointing out the fact that there has been throughout the twentieth century a quiet gnawing at the question, which is quite distinct from those periods when the problem has broken into open dispute. The open disputes have been frequent and intense. Rockefeller money, for example, was first criticized as "tainted," but as we have more reason than many to know the laundering proved to be effective. During both of the world wars and following other episodes of nationalist fervor in the last half century, the conflict between scholarship and citizenship has emerged as an issue. The quieter questioning, however, provides some possible models which may enable us to put the problem in a more systematic context. I would like to describe four such models associated with the history of American social science.

First is the position most closely associated with Thorstein Veblen and the intellectual architects of this building. It argues that the nation's technicians have a knowledge of the industrial-technological system which is a consequence of their special training in the system and which has come to be superior to the knowledge of the entrepreneurs who created the system in the first place. It becomes the responsibility of the new engineers, ultimately, to take over the management of the system, to cease their subservience to their donors, and to undertake a larger responsibility to society as a whole.

Second is the point of view articulated here by Harold Laski in essays written shortly after observing the early programs of the Chicago social scientists and the ambitions of the philanthropists who were funding them. He argued that academics had no essential intellectual relation to their donors and that contact with them and their aims was a danger to the intellectual enterprise. Nor in Laski's terms do academics have basic social responsibilities or even group responsibilities to one another that shape their enterprise. He rejects the concept of teamwork, most of the analogy between social science and natural science, and paints a picture of the isolated intellect pursuing insights to logical conclusions.

Third is the argument posited by Herbert Spencer in the last volume of his *Principles of Sociology*. Spencer traced the academic profession to a priesthood which society was forced to support because of that priesthood's control of communication with the dead. The learned professions in Spencer's analysis continue that reverence for the ultimate truths required by society, not only for the management of daily life but for the very continuity of civilization. Without its priesthood, the donor community would lose touch with its own intellectual reality. Donor gifts to intellectual institutions become celebrations of the donor's moral integrity and responsibility.

Finally, W. I. Thomas, in an essay devoted specifically to an attack on Spencer's position, argues that the learned professions are a consequence of the division of labor, that they come into existence only when those who control society's economic and religious institutions decide they have the time for such pursuits. Thomas even goes so far as to suggest rather pointedly that the recipients are drawn from a lesser order of beings than their donors and that their contributions are basically supports of what their donors have already decided they wish society to know.

In order to keep the distinctions as sharp as possible, we can order them in pairs to suggest similarities and differences. Thus, both Veblen and Spencer emphasize the functional role of intellectuals in relation to donors; but Veblen's intellectuals do not originate the system as Spencer's do. Their knowledge is technical and grows out of the evolution of the system, rather than metaphysical and responsible for the creation of the system. Veblen's engineers are being urged to take over something they did not create, while Spencer's are presumably being pressed to maintain control of something which is fundamentally and originally theirs.

Again, both Veblen and Thomas see the development of the intellectual as a consequence of economic conditions; but Thomas's academics are a lesser order in society which not only cannot but should not have the control Veblen wants them to assert. Both Laski and Thomas see the essential separation between intellectuals and donors, again with a qualitative difference. Laski's intellectuals are more like Spencer's priests, but the separation he calls for is an effort to maintain their intellectual purity. The extremes are Spencer and Thomas, on the one hand, and Veblen and Laski on the other.

For reasons that I think it important to suggest, Americans have preferred to put their arguments in the form of a choice between Veblen and Laski. Thomas and Spencer are most often considered throwbacks to European problems that stretch back even to the much revered antiquity of Athenian political thought. Americans have tended to consider their revolution the beginning or the culmination of a movement that made them independent of the older and starker realities of patronage. The fact that they might not be, or that if they are, there are consequences that ought to be discussed, is really the topic of this paper. Let us begin, then, with the more familiar of the four options, those represented by Veblen and Laski.

Crotchety and cantankerous and highly critical of the roles played by donors and donees in the academic community, Veblen nonetheless managed to describe a model of academic involvement in the world of affairs which comes close to outlining the aims of the generation that built this building. While he castigated the "Captains of Intellect" who managed the university and the academicians who allowed themselves to be bound by their subservience, he also envisioned an alternative role, a leadership that could ultimately be exercised in the places of national power. Not until later in his career did he begin to spell out that role, and then not very clearly. Veblen's engineers could become the benevolent revolutionaries his social thought seemed to require; but only if they came to recognize their ultimate responsibility to lead, to turn their intellects to the management of the social and industrial system, not to the service of its money managers. Those who had made the money would have to turn the system over to those who made it run, because the system ran on knowledge, not on money.

Actually, what Veblen was describing was part of a movement that had begun in the 1880s with the development of the modern professional associations in the social sciences. The young Turks who formed the American Economic Association had tried to persuade their colleagues that their function was to create a socially responsible economics, not one that served the needs of businessmen. Some of the associations sought government charters in order to support their needs for publication. Underneath the association movement, however, was another aim: to free academicians from control by university and college administrators and to give them independent access to the growing sources of funding. By World War I that movement had transformed the funding of academic research. The American Council of Learned Societies and the National Research Council are examples of the mix of public and private funding that emerged as the new academic control of resources for research. The founding of the Social Sciences Research Council and the National Bureau of Economic Research were further steps in the creation of superassociations of scholars with the power to pass judgment on the distribution of resources for research.

By the end of the twenties and before the crash and the depression, the Progressive conception of social science had already begun to achieve status in high places. Herbert Hoover became a champion of the utility of social research for the formulation of social policy. Men like Charles Merriam, William F. Ogburn, and Wesley Clair Mitchell were willing, if not eager, to provide him and his successor with social research on which new social policies might be based. Although it is unlikely that Hoover read Veblen, as an engineer Hoover conceived of himself in near Veblenian terms. There were sciences to consult, sciences which could measure and evaluate social stresses and recommend the necessary restructuring. When such scientists spoke, all reasonable men and women would have to listen. Even politicians would have to listen.

At the University of Chicago, the intimate relation between public policy and social science reached its peak in the 1930s. Though administrators like Robert M. Hutchins were skeptical and willing to say so, the independent access to resources for research achieved by Charles Merriam left such administrators little to do but wield the shovels for the groundbreaking for buildings like this one and 1313 across the midway. The Capitol Limited sped Merriam and his colleagues on their way to Washington and their rooms at the Hay-Adams, the Twentieth Century Limited brought them to the offices of the SSRC on Park Avenue. Throughout the thirties and forties the publication lists of the SSRC included some of the major documents of the period, while the publications of the National Resources Planning Board suggest the effect of growing sums of federal money in the research enterprise. While the competition for resources among the social sciences themselves suggests a certain lack of unanimity, particularly where appointments were concerned, the increased size of the pie made the relative distribution of slices less of a problem.

In the years after World War II the growing federal investment came to dwarf the private resources of the previous decades, but now with an added interest for independent-minded academicians. Professionalization of foundation management, particularly with the entry of the Ford Foundation as a new managerial model, had weakened the control of the academic community itself over the sources of its funding. Government administrators, especially military administrators, seemed much more amenable to advice and much more respectful of independence than the new foundation executives who had disturbing ideas of their own. Many academics began to look to the federal government as the new intellectual democracy. Peer review, administrative laxity, and large amounts of money for which little or no accounting was required were far more attractive. Some even found the growing attacks on foundations rather pleasant, particularly when they were directed at MacGeorge Bundy who appeared to have incurred a large number of debts from liberals and conservatives, politicians and academicians. But that historical moment in 1969 was also another turning point. Vietnam helped foment an intellectual reaction against government that would, I am convinced, have come in any case, although somewhat more slowly. The rapidly expanding government bureaucracy and its at times heavy-handed and politically oriented control over its distribution of resources for research was itself a process that was independent of specific policies.

The problem with the Veblenian model was beginning to become clear, although no one seemed to notice at first. Intellectual control over intellectual life was a lot more tenuous than it appeared in its ideal form. Government bureaus and congressional committees seemed to use ideas, indeed to need ideas. Presidents wanted academic advisors at hand and were willing to scour the academic community in search of them. But funny things happened on the way to the Forum. Ideas, it turned out, were not like medical prescriptions to be taken as directed. Prescriptions could be willfully misused; but the doctor still got the blame. Prescriptions could promise cures that did not exist, could simply turn out to be wrong. Academic malpractice was in the air, and the judgments on academicians who tried to return to the practice of their profession after periods in government posts could be severe. Equally important, everytime the academicians seemed to be approaching their Veblenian goal, something intervened. They had freed themselves from university administrators only to find themselves controlled by foundation administrators. They had freed themselves from foundation administrators to become entrapped by government bureaucrats. Frustrated philosopher-kings, they kept having their thrones pulled out from under them.

Opponents of the Veblenian model were hard put to adopt an independent position, given the dominance of the model throughout the early history of this building. An argument for independence, certainly justifiable in itself, could not be mounted except in opposition; and the results ranged from jocular needling to jugular attack prose, and then silence. President Hutchins helped celebrate the tenth anniversary by asking the celebrants if they thought they had proven they could help the world if they compared conditions in 1939 with conditions in 1929. If there was an answer to his question, it wasn't recorded. President Kimpton asked the twenty-fifth anniversary gathering if they weren't really kidding themselves by calling themselves "scientists" when they were really political opportunists. The editors of that volume buried his welcome in what I'm sure they hoped was the obscurity of the middle of the book. By the 1950s more serious efforts were being made to separate a new discipline called "policy science" from social science as such; but the affluence of the sixties once again blurred the distinction. By the seventies the call for independence was forced to take the form of opposition again, the attack upon intellectuals for having mis-served the state, although some forms of that attack still called for an independent priesthood to criticize policy rather than a separation of intellectual inquiry from any policy aims at all. As important as it ought to be to separate intellectual inquiry from policy, it is a difficult argument to establish as a position apart from the distaste aroused by an era of intense policy involvement. There are reasons for that, and I intend to get them.

One can see at least one articulate statement of opposition produced at the very beginning of this building's history. Harold Laski was one of the most interesting attackers. His collection of essays entitled *The Dangers of Obedience and Other Essays* appeared in 1930. One essay in particular, "Foundations, Universities, and Research," is a criticism of Wesley Clair Mitchell in particular, but of the very concept of social research this building was intended to represent as well. While Laski chose not to hit Merriam or Ogburn or even Chicago by name, he centered on team research, collections of facts, and sending students out on the interview circuit to find out why people didn't vote. The latter point was an obvious reference to one of the most prominent Chicago social research projects of the 1920s.

Laski had three doubts about the whole process of social research in American universities, and they are worth considering. First, he doubted "whether the results to be achieved are likely to be proportionate to the labor involved. I doubt, in the second place," he went on, "whether the effect upon university institutions is likely in the long run to be healthy; and I doubt, in the third place, whether the result of the policy will not be to give the foundations a dominating control over university life which they quite emphatically ought not to have." Laski's first point is the key factor in his intellectual objection to the new conception of social research. He opposed the idea of team or communal research, preferring instead the dependence of intellectual development upon isolated geniuses whose introspective examination of principles gave facts their essential meaning. He also chose to emphasize the role of universities as protective bastions of thought, which needed in turn to be protected from external contacts that might invade or threaten the internal cohesion of the institution. Finally, he saw the external threat posed by the foundation as essentially stupid at worst, second rate intellectually at best. His descriptions of foundation executives are precursors of the typology Dwight MacDonald would later develop in his evolution of the term "Philanthropoid" and, if that is possible, even less sympathetic.

It's important to point out that Laski's conception of the external threat posed by donors is not one that emphasizes a power that is dangerous because it is equal to the internal authority of the university as an institution. This is no Henry-Becket controversy, and certainly no Caesar and God. The external threat is a threat precisely because it is intellectually the lesser of the two, however the more powerful it may be economically. It threatens because it demeans the intellectual integrity of the institution it seeks, from Laski's point of view to corrupt. Even that corruption is not to be viewed as the taking over of one power by another. The children of light are not being conquered by the children of darkness but by dimmer children.

Laski's position leads to another of the basic issues I want to pose. By starting with Veblen and Laski rather than Spencer and Thomas, I specifically wanted to suggest the degree to which the first two are a particularly American method of denying that the other two exist, or that they exist in ways that might make them more relevant to the real facts of donor relationships than Americans like to admit. American intellectuals have shown a greater inclination to define themselves as managers than as priests, not because the role of the priesthood offends them but because American society tends to find managers more acceptable over the long haul than priests. Priests have to commit themselves to ideological positions managers can conceal behind the worship of method. Second, Americans have felt themselves forced to deny that they are simply the servants of those who provide them with their livelihood. While this has long been part of the history of the modern labor movement in the United States, it is an inherent part of the American dilemma of professionalism as well as a problem for those who consider themselves the culture's intellectual leaders. Intellectuals do not wish to acknowledge that they serve their donors, even to the extent of providing them with a dollar's worth of sheer, unintellectual gratification. On those occasions when circumstances force them to acknowledge that they are being fed by a hand, they appear to be professionally committed to biting it.

While there have been American writers who have faced the issue of donor patronage directly, almost all of them have based their arguments on the belief that it ought to be otherwise. The perspectives have been critical, either Veblenian or Marxist. Few American writers have been willing to suggest that the dependence is simply inevitable, to argue that the intellectual professions are inherently dependent upon resources that come from the admittedly more useful economic pursuits and that they exist as gratuitous benefits from willing beneficiaries. I was both fascinated and pleased to run across a significant exception in the history of the social sciences at this university.

The Decennial Publication series that celebrated the tenth birthday of the University of Chicago in 1903 included an essay by W. I. Thomas entitled "The Relations of the Medicine Man to the Origins of the Professional Occupations." It is a curious piece that is more of a fragment than a fully worked-out text. It makes better sense in the form Thomas found for it six years later when he included it in his *Source Book for Social Origins*, along with excerpts from the materials in the third volume of Herbert Spencer's *Principles of Sociology* which it rebuts. Spencer's intellectuals both create and guard the cultural resources of the community. The community needs those resources as necessary elements in its understanding of the relations between life and death and therefore reveres those who control them. Spencer's romantic evolutionism gives intellectuals, then, the most fundamental form of leadership and the most mystical forms of public respect.

Thomas's criticisms are devastating. His argument is worth quoting in full because it rests not only on a clear logical position but on a language that conveys an equally clear judgment.

The most general explanation of the rise of the professional occupations is that they need patronage; and when either the court or the church is developed the patronage is at hand. With the division of labor incident to a growing society, and the consequent increasing irksomeness of labor, particularly of "hard labor," there are always at hand a large number of men to do the less irksome work. Both the hanger-on class and the priest class have, under the patronage of the court and of the church, furthered the development of the learned and artistic professions, and some of the professions have received more encouragement than others from the church because their presence favored the needs and claims of the church. But their development must be regarded as a phase of the division of labor, dependent on economic conditions rather than the presence in society of any particular set of individuals or any peculiar psychic attitude of this set.

The model Thomas is describing leaves little enough room for intellectual heroics, but the language tightens the space even more. The distinction between intellectual activity and "irksome" labor, as well as the references to a class of "hangers-on," puts Spencer's intellectual in their place. It's important to point out that Thomas does not deny the existence of priests or the institution of the church; but he does certainly imply that the initial priests are, like kings, managers who put off the support of intellectual justification until resources are available for such luxuries.

Thomas's point is particularly troublesome in the context of this celebration. Some of the builders of this building were committed to developing a policy-oriented social science. Their patrons most certainly were. Whether social scientists were as clear in their own understanding not only of what they were doing but of what they wanted to do is a matter of some debate, as indeed it always has been. The fact that Thomas's position has been for so many years a near nonexistent one in the academic community might itself be an occasion for debate. Nor are the consequences one can draw from such a debate likely to provoke much agreement. Laski's position is far more attractive. The choice between Veblen and Laski, intellectual conquest or intellectual isolation, has always been more attractive to Americans inured to the belief that it was their responsibility to save the world by conquering it, or to withdraw from it in disdain and isolate their wise innocence from its wickedness. Even Spencer's romanticism has recurrent episodes of popularity for Americans who conceive of their culture as somehow original in its commitment to values the world must learn it needs.

The blunt realism one can extract from Thomas's brief outcry is not very attractive. Social scientists are brought into existence and sustained in their existence by policymakers who find them useful, or at least satisfying in some sense. Intellectuals are not the originators of solutions to the problems posed by material development, however useful they may be in articulating them. In the real world of the division of labor, intellectuals are a dependent class, a luxury class whose labor is less irksome than the labor it takes to make their contribution possible. The consequences of such a point of view for those intellectuals who believe that they have a productive role to play in the formulation of policy are, it seems to me, more complicated than the ironic tone of Thomas's prose might at first suggest.

To return for a moment to the four alternatives I posited at the beginning, it might be useful to reestablish their relation to one another in the context of the discussion up to this point. Thomas's intense materialism is a counter to the teleological purposiveness of Spencer's position, but to Laski's idealistic separatism and Veblen's revolutionary functionalism as well. In its way, Thomas's separatism is as strong as Laski's. While Laski's intellectuals separate to preserve their independence, Thomas's may do the same, acknowledging, of course, that they may starve or, at best, become irrelevant. The intellectuals of Veblen and Spencer may assert their responsibility to influence the direction of policy; but Spencer's do so as an original right due them by their access to the higher order of knowledge, while Veblen's must assume the responsibility of creating a revolution that will put their superior knowledge in charge.

All four positions can be seen as efforts to define a relation between the responsibilities of the citizen and the responsibilities of the scholar in relation to the state. While the shift in language may complicate the discussion a bit, it may also help clarify the basic and most philosophical issues the argument was intended to debate. The relation between intellectuals and their donors has always been a variant of the relation between intellectuals and the state. For a crucial period of modern American history, roughly the scant century between the years immediately after the Civil War and the recent past, donor support of intellectual life in the

United States did not come from a national government or a national economic elite whose relation to the national government was clear. Even state and local governments which did support educational and cultural institutions did so with a large mixture of private support and with an overriding commitment to practicality and democratic utility. Even when one acknowledges periodic flurries of donor concern with radicalism and supposed un-American teaching, American intellectual institutions remained remarkably free of intervention by the state throughout the century of their most dramatic expansion. At the same time, a great number of American intellectuals deliberately sought intervention in policymaking at all levels of government and fought successfully to create a system in which their intellectual institutions would accept the responsibility of protecting them from the critical attacks their interventions would provoke from time to time. The very meaning of academic freedom was transformed. What once had been the freedom from having to serve the state in particular ways became the freedom to serve the state or criticize it, either one with impunity. Trustees who had once sought to have faculty members fired for opposing national monetary policy found by the New Deal that they were equally offended by scholars who were providing Roosevelt with supportive arguments for policies they also opposed. By the 1950s presidents of the major private universities had grown accustomed to defending faculties against outside attacks from government and inside attacks from disgruntled trustees and alumni. State institutions bowed to legislatures that required loyalty oaths; but faculties throughout the so-called McCarthy era responded with a remarkable and disturbing self-restraint, rendering unto Caesar by trying to behave like Caesar's wife. When national policy began to disturb the academic community in the mid-sixties it was the recollection of the previous decade that spurred the new activism for many of the older participants. Yet the Vietnam era, despite its intensity, demonstrated a protection that by standards of any previous era was extraordinary. While private universities suffered a certain amount of donor resentment, the degree of direct attack by critics in government, the press, or the power elite in industry simply bore little relation to similar efforts at reprisal in the fifties, and certainly not to the degree of provocation being generated by academic behavior. Indeed, one could argue that the most painful wounds and the most lasting scars were those we inflicted on one another. The young we taught, a generation for whom the fifties was infancy, suffered far more from the decisions they were forced to make than did the tenured faculties who sympathized with them. It was the students who found themselves faced with the choice of martyrdom or flight.

Both eras, however, raised one of the essential historic relationships, and the comparison between the two suggests that there have been changes that ought to be explored. Historically the relation between the scholar and the citizen has been a troubled one, the subject of discussions about the origins of revolution, the stability or instability of political regimes, and, above all, the most dangerous thing intellectuals have been perceived historically to engage in: the teaching of the young. That may be why some of us try to avoid teaching, or do it as casually as we can, pretending that it really isn't as important as our research. As far back at least as Socrates, intellectuals sought to establish a relationship between their responsibilities to the teaching of the truth and their responsibilities to the state. Socrates's answer, which for years we have taught as one of the Great Books of Western Civilization, was that our duty to the state ultimately required us to accept martyrdom if necessary, but in support of the state, not in revolutionary opposition to it. He refused to seek asylum, to defect, to hide. For years commentators recounted Aristotle's response to a similar crisis—he fled, lest Athens sin twice against philosophy the legend goes. He was cited to indicate his cowardice, a contrast with Socrates' bravery.

One need not question our defense of our right to truth in the face of attack by the state or rejection by donors to ask if we are really thinking about the consequences of what in fact is a genuine historical change. If scholarship is independent of citizenship and prior to it, if those upon whom we depend for financial support have no authority to criticize what we do, and if these are commitments we are teaching to the young, what social consequences are we likely to produce? We can argue that we are not in the business of producing social consequences and let it go at that. Or we can suggest that we are really revolutionaries and get on with our revolution, being aware, of course, that, as the Russians and the Chinese have so brilliantly demonstrated, revolutionaries have to have a means of maintaining loyalty to the revolution, and the individual's defense of truth is not at the top of the list.

American intellectuals appear to have won a centuries-old battle for independence. They have achieved a freedom to dissent and have protected their rights to be just as hostile as they have wanted to be. Several of the government-sponsored Jefferson lecturers have celebrated their liberty by making their well-dressed audiences as uncomfortable as well-dressed people ever get, a tweak here, a pinch there, and one or two deft belts to the old gizoo. When William Simon recently suggested that donors ought not support institutions that taught principles they didn't agree with, he was greeted like a serpent in the academic garden selling apples. The problem, of course, is that we are no longer innocent, if indeed we ever were. We have a taste for the fruit of the tree of knowledge, and we can't be expelled from our gardens.

A recurrent theme in recent academic literature defines the intellectual now as social critic, but in a sense that differs significantly from the critical stances implied by the four models. Each of the four holds as fundamental assumption the belief that academics are citizens of the larger societies in which their institutions exist. Those societies are the traditional national entities of our historic past. Spencer's priests may, one assumes, feel called upon to act as Jeremiahs, but their criticisms would appear to be based on shared religious beliefs that give them the responsibility of bringing the larger society back to the paths from which it has strayed. Veblen's engineers are committed to changing the path; but once they have changed it their superior management should lessen the need for criticism in what, for American social critics of Veblen's generation, was always some form of restoration to original American principles of economic and political behavior. Laski's academicians, certainly the most classically monastic of the four, were still impacted in a traditional British context Laski and the London School of Economics were seeking to transform. The somewhat puzzling supine realism of Thomas's position is made less puzzling, perhaps, by what happened to Thomas in the course of his career, his expulsion from this university and his acceptance of that expulsion, apparently, as his lot in life. During the First World War Thomas was accused of violating the Mann Act with the wife of an army officer from Indiana. Defenders of Thomas believed the story to have been a "sting" set up by wartime critics of Mrs. Thomas's pacifist activities; but wartime hysteria and newspaper agitation pressed the university to hasty action. Recent investigators starting with recent conceptions of academic freedom as a legally defensible right have found it difficult to understand. Neither Thomas nor his colleagues seriously fought his firing. The board of the university press protested the action of the trustees in withdrawing Thomas's publications with such ruthless abruptness; but it seems to have been the fact that they did it without consultation that upset the members of the press board, not any question of their right to take the actions they took. Academicians of that generation accepted institutional authorities of various kinds. They fought to establish independence, not dominance, and the distinction is important.

The two decades since 1960 have witnessed a remarkable shift in the public's perception of the roles played by academics in national life as well as in the American academic's perception of that role. John F. Kennedy's charge to the country's university elite ran from the professors he called to Washington not only to advise but to manage, to the bright-eyed students he sent in Peace Corps battalions throughout the world. Revelations of academic involvement in the planning of Cold War strategies, the responsibilities of the so-called best and brightest for decisions regarding Vietnam, and the engagement of academics in covert intelligence work all produced a reaction that led writers like Christopher Lasch to posit a new role for the nation's intellectuals.

The responsibility of the intellectuals, it has been argued, is to truths embodied in the pursuit of knowledge and the professions that support that pursuit. Such truths transcend nationality and patriotism. Knowledge is the responsibility of the community that produces it and determines its quality. Such arguments are not necessarily new. They echo, certainly, some aspects of Spencer's position; but they can be found as well in Thomas Jefferson's assertions of the justification for revolution. Support of the rights of man against encroachment by the state is well within our national traditions, as is the dependence on truths held to be self-evident. But there is one essential difference. Jefferson assumed a transfer of allegiance from a nation-state that refused to respect rights to one that did. The present arguments have a different quality to them. In fields as widely separated on the intellectual spectrum as physics and ballet, individuals are insisting upon their right to pursue their professions and defining that right as one which is prior to the demands or needs of any state. Allegiance to profession has become prior to allegiance to state. Intellectuals are declaring what may well be a new independence.

American academia has internationalized far more rapidly since the end of World War II than it had in the decades that preceded the war, although the process of intellectual internationalization goes back to our national origins. Despite nationalist efforts to keep science and technology contained, they have proved themselves inherently independent of national interest when that interest was perceived as restrictive and protective. The initial celebration of the opening of this building was designed as an international event, far more so than any of the subsequent anniversary celebrations and certainly more than this one. The reason may not be any stepping away from internationalism but simply the acceptance of it as a fact that no longer has to be promoted.

At the same time, that internationalization means that American academia is no longer the nationalist community it was in the thirties and forties. Nor is that a condition that can be ascribed necessarily to either liberalism or conservatism, a factor which is also new. Our commitments to truth as we understand it in science, to art as it is accepted internationally, and to our rights to pursue our individual careers in either area unfettered by service to the state requires us to become social critics or to claim the right of total withdrawal from nationalist society without loss of livelihood, surely the ultimate defection.

Martyrdom, in the classical sense of the term applicable to either Socrates or W. I. Thomas, no longer holds the meaning it has had for centuries. We know that it played a crucial role in the development of Western thought. It served to sustain unpopular ideas until they became popular, to provide unbelievers with heroes in whom to believe, and to create myths capable of persuading generations to persist in their support of eccentric aims. While its decline is not an unmixed blessing, our ability to protect ourselves from it has consequences which, like the decline in academic nationalism, ought to be examined. Our belief in ourselves as citizens of no other community than our own professions—and the insistence among some of us of the right to dissent even from that community's demands—is bound to affect the way other communities look at us, and that must include the majorities for whom citizenship and national interest are still core elements. We may believe we have restricted their power to martyr us, but we cannot prevent them from ignoring us. That, in the long run, may do more to shape our future than anything else. If Thomas's insight is really at the center of any definition of our relationship to those who support our enterprise, it ought to be taken more seriously than we have been inclined to take it and its implications examined. The seventy-fifth anniversary of this building might call for an entirely different kind of celebration.

9 Distortions of Economic Research

Theodore W. Schultz

UNIVERSITY OF CHICAGO

I feel sure you have a little list of economic distortions that you would gladly see put underground. I am aware there are social scientists who are sure that economists debase social and cultural values in their monolithic concentration on economic values, that they neglect methodology, that they disregard social behavior that is deemed to be inconsistent with the rationality assumptions of economic theory, and that they have a penchant to be imperialistic. Scientists also are uneasy about the economists' treatment of the choices of human agents in the context of scarcity. The National Academy of Sciences looks with favor on economists who reveal some mathematical elegance, but it is uncomfortable about economic criticism of the work that the NAS does on request for the U.S. government. Governments are most uneasy unless economists are beholden to them and provide support for their economic policies. The intellectual fashion at present is research on current economic policy regardless of how politicized and transitory the issues are.

The distortions in economic research, which I shall feature, are not a consequence of the reservations that the other social scientists have about economic research. The distortions on my list have come about mainly because of the economic policy biases of some foundations and of most governmental agencies in allocating funds for economic research and because of the accommodations of a goodly number of academic economists to these biases in order to obtain research funds.

Economists have prospered from a long boom for their services. The demand for economic research has increased at a rapid

I am indebted to Zvi Griliches, D. Gale Johnson, William H. Kruskal, and T. Paul Schultz for their helpful suggestions and critical comments. A somewhat reduced version was published in *Minerva* 17, no. 3 (1979):460–68. Reprinted with permission.

pace largely as a consequence of the research activities of new institutions. These institutions are in the ascendancy in competing for research funds, and in this competition the comparative advantage of university research is declining. Foundations have contributed somewhat to this new pattern in economic research; however, the increases in federal research funds are vastly more important in financing this development. One of the salient attributes of booms is that they tend to produce distortions, and on this score economic research has not been spared. From an academic viewpoint, disconcerting changes in the demand for economic research are clearly evident, and they favor strongly new types of institutes that serve the policy interests of governmental agencies. These have grown like Topsy. I am concerned about the adverse effects of this development on the research and the educational functions of academic economists.

Patrons of university activities are not renowned for their neutrality when it comes to economic research. Politicized economic research has become the order of the day. It is evident in the "targeted research" and the "mission oriented research" objectives that have become enshrined in most projects that are funded by governmental agencies and also in some foundation grants. Nor are private patrons innocent in this respect.

My purpose is to question society's institutions that allocate funds to universities for economic research. It entails an examination of the distortions in the educational and research functions which are in substantial measure consequences of society's institutions. It also calls for a critique of the functions of university economists.

Institutions Involved in Economic Research

I do not want to imply that all economic research prior to two or three decades ago was being done by universities. Large business firms, including banks and trade associations, have been employing economists for many decades to do research deemed to be useful to them. Organized labor and national farm organizations have done likewise, especially so beginning with the New Deal era. There are also bureaus of long standing, staffed with competent economists, in the federal departments of agriculture, commerce, labor, and the treasury that have been and continue to be engaged in the measurement of economic components and in producing economic statistics. Among the early not-for-profit pioneers, two are noteworthy. The National Bureau of Economic Research, guided at the outset by the distinguished economist Wesley Mitchell, did yeoman work. The NBER sought the assistance and criticism of university economists. It engaged in measurement and in producing data that required facilities and staff that no university could afford. The remarkable research of Simon Kuznets and his associates for the NBER developed the concepts and the measurements that are requied in national income accounting. Currently, however, the research of the NBER is largely devoted to current policy issues, and it has become substantially dependent on public funds. The Brookings Institution, which is the other major, long-established research organization, has been much favored by foundation grants and also by public funds. During its early years under the leadership of Harold Moulton, and at times since then, a good deal of the economic research of Brookings has been closely identified with that of particular current policy objectives.

The other research entities that have been less well known are the following: the National Planning Association, which dates back to the New Deal period, has been over the years strongly policy oriented. Following World War II, the Committee for Economic Development, in protest to the dominant views of business organizations, contributed substantially in clarifying some of the then policy issues. Each of the long-established twelve Federal Reserve Banks has a research department headed by a vice-president. The economic staff in the systems headquarters in Washington is large. Most of the research of the Federal Reserve system, however, is confined to in-house purposes, and all too few of their studies are published in professional journals. For a few years while C. O. Hardy was at Kansas City Bank it was an exception, and more recently the St. Louis Federal Reserve Bank has also been an exception.

During the past twenty-five years the proliferation of institutes engaged in economic research has been extraordinary. They have emerged, as already noted, in response to the availability of the large increases in funds for specific economic policy research. A drastic shift has occurred in the allocation of research funds in favor of those that specialize in the appropriate research and that are not encumbered by being too closely connected with a university. Some on-campus institutes that are not hampered by the academic duties of departments of economics have been favored. In large measure this shift has come about because most university departments of economics are deemed to be too rigid, because they resist interdisciplinary and team research projects, and because they are too committed to on-going traditional Ph.D. research, to theoretical studies, and to esoteric empirical work. Moreover, universities in large measure are viewed as being either unable or unwilling to shape up and do the type of policy research that is wanted.

Following World War II nonprofit research institutes have become a robust growth industry. We now have all manner of institutes with much specialization. The list is indeed long: over three hundred in economics research.[1] There are institutes that specialize in economic development, econometric models, international trade, taxation, enterprise, education, urban development, energy, manpower, consumer affairs, environmental reforms, legal issues, health, population, and in poverty. Nor are the research funds for these purposes small; for example, the federal government is allocating approximately $90 million a year to support poverty research.[2] Since the growth of this industry has occured predominantly outside of the confines of the universities, the implication is that university economic research has not satisfied this specialized demand for economic research.

Clearly some private patrons of economic research, foundations, and virtually all governmental agencies have decided that universities lack the capacity or the desire to do the research that they demand. Having made this decision, it is obvious that other options would be pursued. One option that has been pursued by some foundations is to undertake and manage as an in-house activity the research they want. It is a way of establishing new policy areas that then serve to determine the type of grant propo-

1. Archie M. Palmer, ed., *Research Centers Directory*, 6th ed. (Detroit: Gale Research Co. 1979), lists 304 nonprofit research organizations in the United States and Canada engaged in economic research. Many of them have some sort of affiliation with a university.
    2. National Research Council, National Academy of Sciences, *Evaluating Federal Support of Poverty Research* (Boston: G. K. Hall & Co., 1979 [cloth]; Cambrige, Mass.: Schenkman Publishing Co., 1979 [paper]).

sals that will be considered. In a variant of this option, the Carnegie Foundation established the Carnegie Commission on Higher Education and allocated some millions of dollars to this endeavor. The Ford Foundation's first in-house report on energy, *A Time to Choose* (1974), is an example of harmful economic policy advocacy befitting a populist approach in coping with the energy problems. The third Ford Foundation (1979) in-house report, *Energy: The Next Twenty Years*, prepared under the direction of Hans H. Landsberg, makes a good deal of economic sense. The funding of new research institutes is the option that has been pursued on a grand scale. A few of them are doing first-rate research, producing analytical studies of high quality. A notable example is the performance over the past twenty-five years of Resources for the Future, a relatively small institute that concentrates on studies pertaining to natural resources and, although natural resources are a highly sensitive political area, the research of RFF has not become dependent on government project funds and it has successfully resisted a foundation effort to bring about a "forced marriage" between RFF and another much larger institution that has the proper policy qualifications.

The Office of Naval Analysis and Air Force Project Rand supported significant work in mathematical and theoretical economics during the 1950s and 1960s. Doctoral and postdoctoral research in human capital was broadly supported by the National Institute of Mental Health during the 1970s, when it was abruptly terminated because it was then deemed to be not sufficiently applied, given the legal mandate of NIMH. Earlier, research in agriculture economics at the University of Chicago and Harvard University, supported by USDA funds, was also terminated abruptly, in this case because of the whims of the chairman of a congressional appropriation committee. The majority of Congress tend to be opposed to having governmental agencies allocate research funds to economists who are presumed to be critical of particular public programs.

Up to this point I have featured the dynamics of the recent proliferation of economic research. No doubt a good deal of this research is useful in serving the specific purposes of the patrons who provide the funds. As a by-product, some of the new institutes contribute occasionally to the advancement of economics. But the success of these new institutes does not resolve the question whether or not academic economic thought and research is useful in determining the merits and limitations of economic policies. I shall deal with that question later. The primary thrust of my argument thus far is that the professional personnel who manage the governmental agencies that allocate research funds under the restrictions imposed by Congress are constrained and thus not free, leaving aside the issue of the required competence, to determine the type of university support that would serve the proper function of academic economists. Although the National Science Foundation may be viewed as an exception, all too few NSF grants support criticism of the state of economic analysis. Despite the trying political opposition to economics, NSF has supported the research of Nelson and Winter criticizing the profit-maximizing analysis of the behavior of firms, Fogel's attack on society's institutions, and Lucas's criticism of existing macro-orthodoxy. The distortions about which we should be concerned also entail the accommodations that are made by universities to obtain research funds from foundations, from government, and from the new breed of institutes when they offer to subcontract some of their on-going research.

In questioning society's institutions, there have been tensions between what economists do and what the dominant institutions of society want them to do that antedate by centuries the current period. The differences in basic economic issues were as pervasive then as the tensions associated with the recent developments on which I have dwelt.

Questioning Society's Institutions

Economists have long been critics of society's institutions. Historically economists have criticized the economic doctrines of the church, the state, the property ownership class (landlords), and the mercantile doctrine, among others. Although the state of this uneasiness between these institutionalized doctrines and economic thought has a long history, the nature of the difficulties has changed over time. The scholarly studies of Jacob Viner feature the economic doctrines of the early Christian fathers, of the Scholastics, of the secularizing tendencies in Catholic social thought, and of Protestantism and the rise of capitalism.[3] The

3. Jacob Viner, *Religious Thought and Economic Society*, four chaps. of an unfinished work edited by Jacques Melitz and Donald Winch (Durham, N.C.: Duke University Press, 1978).

doctrines of the church pertaining to usury, to the sterility of money capital and the just price are examined in the context of the then prevailing scholarship. There is also the critical essay by Viner, "The Role of Providence in the Social Order."[4] While the tensions between religious and economic thought have declined, some differences persist on particular social and economic issues inherent in the doctrines pertaining to the relationships between church and state.

The remarkable decline in rent from land relative to the earnings of labor and other sources of income in the high-income countries has very much reduced the social and political influence of landlords, and the tensions between them and economic thought have diminished as a consequence. Meanwhile, however, some of the economic entitlements that business firms, organized labor, organized agricultural, and organized environmental groups demand, strain the relationship between them and economics.

We are in an era in which the tensions between the university and the state have become increasingly acute. These difficulties are not restricted to private universities nor are they specific to the United States. They are worldwide, although they differ greatly among the more than 150 nation-states. In most nations the intellectual independence of the university is seriously constrained, especially so in the case of social and economic thought and research. What these nation-states want makes this relationship fragile and subjects it to much uncertainty for universities. It is true even in the United States that the more heavily the university is dependent on the patronage of government, the less is the freedom of inquiry in the social sciences.

Throughout much of the world, what academic economists do is decidedly beholden to governments. It is obviously so in the Soviet Union, China, and in the other countries that have centralized the control of their economy. Meanwhile many low-income countries have opted for a partially controlled economy and for external subsidies to equalize the differences in per capita income between them and the rich countries. It is presumed that academic economists can, once they are required to do so, rationalize these objectives. Tensions have also increased during

4. Jacob Viner, *The Role of Providence in the Social Order: An Essay in Intellectual History* (Philadelphia, Pa: American Philosophical Society, 1972 [cloth]; Princeton, N.J.: Princeton University Press, 1976 [paper]).

recent decades on issues pertaining to economic policy in Western Europe and North America, where democratic governments have long prevailed.

I believe it is fair to say that within the university economics is much more vulnerable to off-campus intrusions than university research in the natural sciences. The vulnerability of biological research to governmental regulation, however, has become serious, but even at that economics is decidedly more exposed to subversion. I hasten to acknowledge that recent antiscience movements are changing the relationship between science and the public perception of the sciences, and in this process these movements have to some extent politicized the allocation of public funds for science research. Edward Shils has dealt thoughtfully with this issue in his essay, "Faith, Utility and the Legitimacy of Science."[5] Would that there were a comparable essay on the utility of economics.

A Modest Critique of Academic Economics

Despite inflation and the university's financial stringency, academic economists have not fared badly in large part because of the nonuniversity market for the services of economists. By this market test it would be all too easy to conclude that economists are highly productive of something that the university or society want. But in fact the utility that either the university or society derives from what academic economists do is not obvious. While economists are not reluctant to ascertain the value derived from the use of scarce resources by people in any other activity, they are shy when it comes to reckoning the utility of their own work. It is my contention that most academic economists are complacent about their freedom of inquiry, about safeguarding their university functions, and about the conditions under which research funds are made available to them by institutions other than the university. This complacency about the special and specific usefulness of inquiry that is free of outside intrusion is exemplified in their failure to challenge publicly private patrons, foundations, and governmental agencies on their allocation of funds for economic research. But to do this competently requires firm knowledge of the utility of economic thought

5. Edward Shils, "Faith, Utility and the Legitimacy of Science," in *Science and Its Public: The Changing Relationship, Daedalus* (Summer 1974).

and research appropriate to the functions of the university. It also requires courage, because it entails the risk of alienating the patrons and causing them to reduce further their support of university research. This risk is neatly avoided by the art of accommodation, by quietly and gracefully submitting proposals for research grants that seem to fit the demands of the patrons.

Suffice it to say that economics deals with a mundane part of human activities. It is useful to the extent that it is practical. Its utility is not in its beauty, which it lacks, nor in the elegance of its mathematics. The fundamentals of economics are useful in both private and public affairs and especially so in determining the economic consequences of public policies, which is the essence of the domain of political economy, and which is featured in the title of our professional journal at the University of Chicago (*Journal of Political Economy*).

According to my critique, the distinction between the concepts of applied and basic research is not meaningful in determining the function of academic economics. The now fashionable concepts of targeted and mission-oriented research are as a rule subterfuges for intrusion. Peer review of economic research proposals by individuals who are selected by the granting agency, notably so in the case of some governmental agencies, is a convenient device for obtaining sufficient differences in evaluations to give the administrator of the agency a free hand in deciding whether or not to approve the proposal. Turning to the positive function of academic economists, its forte is in comprehensive analysis and criticism of private economic behavior and of public policies. Comprehensiveness in this context does not restrict academic economics to improvements of the internal consistency of economic logic and thereby making it more rigorous, nor does it limit economics to advances in quantitative analytical tools and improvements in empirical analysis, although these endeavors are exceedingly important. To be comprehensive, academic economists cannot divorce themselves from the social attributes of society and from the insights of the humanities and of history. Hayek[6] could say with good grace what he said at our twenty-fifth year celebration, "Nobody can be a great economist who is only an economist," and he added "that an economist who is only an

6. F. A. Hayek, "The Dilemma of Specialization," in *The State of the Social Sciences*, ed. Leonard Dupee White (Chicago: University of Chicago Press, 1956).

economist is likely to become a nuisance if not a positive danger." It is my contention that the "Dilemma of Specialization" remains unresolved.

One of the primary functions of at least a subset of economists, whose freedom of inquiry is protected by their university, is to devote their talent to comprehensive social and economic criticism. Scholarly criticism of economic doctrines and society's institutions by economists is at a low ebb—criticism, for example, of the quality of the work of Jacob Viner, Frank Knight, and Harry Johnson, and also of Thorstein Veblen, Henry Simon, and Friedrich A. Hayek, all of whom were members of the faculty of this university. It is noteworthy that the studies and publications of only one of this group was supported by foundations, governmental agencies, or by private patrons. I find it highly unlikely that university economists of their caliber and with their scholarly interest could today obtain funds from off-campus sources. But what is also distressing is that the search for talent is for a different set of economic qualifications, and as a consequence there is a lack of incentives for the on-coming generation of economists to acquire the competence that is required to pursue scholarly criticism of economic doctrines and of society's institutions. It is my contention that one of the primary functions of at least a subset of economists, whose freedom of inquiry is protected by their university, is to devote their talent to comprehensive social and economic criticism.

The criticism that is lacking is fairly obvious. There are all too few competent critical studies of the economic doctrines of the host of United Nations' organizations, despite the fact that most of them are debasing economics. Whereas the early economic doctrines of the Church were supported, as Viner has shown, by considerable scholarship, the economic doctrines that prevail within the United Nations are not burdened by scholarship. It is to the lasting credit of Harry Johnson that he did challenge these doctrines.[7] Peter Bauer of the London School of Economics is another exception in his dissent on economic development doctrines.[8] The pronounced drift toward soft economics by some of

7. Harry G. Johnson, *On Economics and Society* (Chicago: University of Chicago Press, 1975).
8. P. T. Bauer, *Dissent on Development*, Studies and Debates in Development Economics (Cambridge, Mass.: Harvard University Press, 1972).

the foundations goes unchallenged by economists. This adverse drift is in large measure a consequence of a "live and let live" policy which requires accommodation to demands of the prevailing international organizations and to the current politicized demands within the United States.

In analyzing choices and scarcities, economists tend to hold fast to the preferences of individuals and families, including the preferences that are served by household activities. Some of society's institutions, however, distort these preferences. There is a pervasive intellectual and popular commitment to the belief that the failures of the market are the primary source of what is wrong with the economy. Each interest group has its own agenda of such market failures. To overcome them, an increasing number of organized groups seek protection and redress by means of public programs and institutions created by government. Business groups have a long history of serving their special interest by this means. Organized labor and organized commodity groups have been doing this on behalf of their special interests for decades. This pluralistic process is currently confounded by the politics of health, of the aged, of poverty, of income transfers, of energy, of environmental politics, and others. The resulting modifications of the political economy in general do not correct actual market failures but tend to bring about other forms of economic failures. My concern on this point is that, in part by design but mainly unwittingly, some of the specialized research in departments of economics supports this special interest fragmentation of the economy by means of governmental intervention. Surely, it is not the function of academic economists to contribute to such fragmentation of the political economy. This type of distortion of economic research is in some measure induced the conditions attached to the research funds that are available to academic economists.

Economic research in most universities is less than optimum for several additional reasons. Ph.D. research in general is not well organized. There is a lack of opportunities for graduate students to make progress reports on their research at regularly scheduled meetings organized to provided useful criticism by other graduate students and faculty. Members of the faculty who are in charge of supervising Ph.D. research are frequently involved in off-campus consulting to private business and government agencies. Such consulting can divert their intellectual endeavors from research that is appropriate to the functions of the universities.[9] Although the administration and faculty of universities proclaim that research is one of their major and vital functions, the bureaucratic financial organization of the university provides little direct support for economic research. This financial issue is more acute in economics than in the sciences. Economics does not require laboratories and expensive physical facilities. All an empirical economist needs is a research assistant, perhaps a programmer, access to a suitable computer, and funds to acquire data. The effects of this unsolved university problem on the incentives of academic economists are beset with distortions.

Concluding Remark

The charters of our not-for-profit foundations do not require that they support primarily all manner of short-range, politicized economic policy research. Foundations have on occasion provided funds for comprehensive, long-range, policy research. The Rockefeller Foundation, for example, has generously funded the agricultural economics workshop at this university continuously since the early forties. At an earlier period the Rockefeller Foundation on its own initiative offered the Ames group of economists a generous grant without any restrictions on the range of policy issues that would be investigated. I would be less than grateful if I did not acknowledge the six recent years of support I received from the Ford Foundation for research and writing of my own choosing. There are of course other examples of this type of support by foundations. The secular drift, however, as I have argued, has been to support the wide array of new institutes that specialize on current, short-range, economic policy issues.

Government agencies, however, do not have the freedom that

9. While I am uneasy about some aspects of this consulting, the evidence reported by Carl V. Patton and James D. Marver suggests that from 1969 to 1975 there has not been any increase in academic consulting. The evidence also indicates, controlling for type of institution and rank of faculty, that paid consultants do somewhat more research, more graduate instruction, publish more, and more of them serve as chairmen of departments than do those faculty who are not paid consultants. See their "Paid Consulting by American Academics," *Educational Record* 60 (Spring 1979), pp. 175–84; and an earlier paper by them, "The Correlates of Consultation: American Academics in the 'Real World,'" *Higher Education* (August 1976), pp. 319–35.

foundations have when it comes to providing funds for comprehensive economic policy research. These agencies are constrained by congressional mandates that determine the research purposes to which federal funds can be put. The National Science Foundation has more degrees of freedom than other government agencies, but it too is hampered by some particular short-range tests of useful research imposed by Congress. It must be said that Congress has wantonly politicized the policy research of the vast number of administrative units of government that have been established to promulgate the declared policies mandated by Congress. The politics of research is bad for economic research. Whereas the funds authorized by Congress for research are large, in allocating these funds virtually every administrative agency of government is restricted to research that will support its particular policy mandate. It is not within the domain of the agency to finance competent economic criticism of the agency's activities or of the adverse effects of economic policy fragmentation.

Federal research funds have not always been allocated in this perverse manner. The Purnell Act is a clear case of federal funding of university research that has had continuity and stability, sufficiently so to make tenure appointments. It is now fifty years ago that the Purnell Act authorized an annual appropriation of $60,000 (read $250,000 in 1979 prices) for each of the land grant universities to be used for rural social science research.[10] Agricultural economics is the primary recipient of these federal funds. These funds provide continuing core support for faculty and Ph.D. research. This research is not beholden to the federal government, although it has not always been free of political intrusions on the part of the states.

The core of my argument is that one of the primary functions of academic economists is to question society's institutions. Economists are all too complacent about their freedom of inquiry. They are not sufficiently vigilant in safeguarding their function as educators. They should give a high priority to scholarly criticism of economic doctrines and of society's institutions. The distortions of economic research will not fade away by accommodating patrons of research funds.

10. Theodore W. Schultz, with the assistance of Lawarence W. Witt, *Training and Recruiting of Personnel in the Rural Social Studies* (Washington, D.C.: American Council on Education, 1941).

10 Federal Support in the Social Sciences

Richard C. Atkinson
NATIONAL SCIENCE FOUNDATION

The debate regarding the federal role in the support of social science research is long-standing and tends to intensify at this time of year as Congress begins its annual examination of the President's budget. There are supporters of the social sciences in Congress, but there are also vigorous critics. Criticism follows two contradictory lines of argument. In the first, social science research is regarded as irrelevant to societal needs and, therefore, a waste of taxpayers' dollars. The contrary argument is that the social sciences are all too relevant—leading to social engineering and manipulation of moral values—and should not be encouraged, let alone supported. Both of these views create difficulties for those who argue for increased support for social science research.

How has this debate affected federal funding for the social sciences? The facts are surprising. As a percent of the federal budget for both basic and applied research, the social sciences— defined in the National Science Foundation data base as anthropology, economics, political sciences, geography, and sociology—have remained remarkably constant at 5 percent of the total for well over a decade. A somewhat different picture emerges, however, if one examines where the research is performed (in colleges and universities, independent nonprofit organizations, industry, or government laboratories). Consider, for example, federal funds for basic research. Across all fields of science, the percentage of basic research performed at academic institutions has been roughly constant at 48 percent since 1973—the first years such data were collected. In contrast, 60 percent of basic research in the social sciences was performed at academic institutions in 1973, but that number had decreased to 47 percent by 1978. The cumulative impact is significant: from

Reprinted with permission from *Science*, vol. 207, 22 February 1980, p. 829.

1973 to 1979, federal funds for basic research at colleges and universities in all scientific fields increased 97 percent; in social sciences the increase was 37 percent. The same trends hold for federally supported applied research and for the composite of basic and applied research.

Setting aside questions about the classification of basic and applied research and possible spillovers from developmental work, these data indicate a shift of social science research away from academic institutions. We will have to know more about the nonacademic performers and the research they are doing before the trends can be interpreted. We do know that the job market is a factor. Although faculty positions in the social sciences have increased at about the same rate as the average for all fields of science, the number of new social science Ph.D.'s requires that many seek employment outside universities. Another factor may be that federal agencies are exercising more control over the content and climate of research. Professor Theodore Schultz, the University of Chicago's most recent Nobel Laureate in Economics, has commented on the distortions in economic research introduced by the influence of patrons—federal and private—and the resultant decline in academic research with no readily apparent utility. Constrained by the criticisms mentioned above, funding agencies may be trying to ensure that the relevance of the social science they support is easily justified and, at the same time, poses no threat to society's values.

The shift away from academia in the social sciences has consequences for graduate education, for methodological work, and for the balance between fundamental and policy-oriented research. A case can be made that the shift has been beneficial for certain specialties and has strengthened links between academia and the real world. Whatever the judgment, it is important that we be aware of what is taking place and consider the consequences in planning for the future.

11 Discrepancies Between Concepts and Their Measurements: The Urban-Rural Example

Norman M. Bradburn
UNIVERSITY OF CHICAGO

Social scientists face a dilemma. The problems they study are understood in familiar terms. Yet, if in their investigations, they use familiar terms for social phenomena to which they give precise or special meanings, they risk being misunderstood. Familiar terms carry with them many vague, imprecise connotations. If social scientists resort to new or unfamiliar terms, they are accused of using jargon or giving fancy names to commonplace events.

Investigators who steer for the Scylla of ordinary language concepts rather than the Charybdis of technical terms have the further problem of insuring a decent fit between their own conceptual definitions of terms and the measures that are employed to give empirical meaning to those terms. They must confront the problem of moving from a conceptual definition used in a theory and couched in familiar terms to a definition based on the measurement operations used to provide data by which the investigators' ideas about the relationships among their concepts can be tested. If the measurement process distorts the intended meaning of the concepts, then the ideas cannot be validly tested. The difficulty in formulating adequate measures for familiar concepts has led some investigators to reject the notion that they can be measured at all. Perhaps a more common response today is to reject the use of familiar terms, using instead technical terms which take their meanings from the measures by which they are defined.

In this paper I shall pursue the relation between two social science concepts that are expressed in ordinary language words and the way in which they are measured. These concepts are "urban" and "rural." They are particularly fitting to consider in a symposium dedicated to the fiftieth anniversary of the opening of the Social Science Research Building, because they are terms that have figured prominently in the development of the social sciences at the University of Chicago. The urban-rural dichotomy, with particular emphasis on the urban side, has been associated with much of the historically prominent work at Chicago in anthropology, sociology, political science, and geography. The names of Redfield, Park, Wirth, Gosnell, and Mayer, to name but a few, are familiar to all who have looked into social science literature on urban life. In fact two papers given in this room almost exactly forty years ago, papers by Merriam and Wirth, were devoted to urbanism (Wirth 1940).

That we live in an urban society is a fact known to all. That we are more urbanized now than we were in the eighteenth century is obvious without laborious reference to statistics, although a determination of just how much more urbanized we are now requires some measurement. Whether this situation reflects a trend that is increasing, decreasing, or has halted requires much more serious attention to measurement problems. In *Historical Statistics of the United States* (U.S. Bureau of the Census 1975) we find that 5.1 percent of the population was urban in 1800. By 1900 the proportion had grown to 39.7 percent. In 1970 it was 73.5 percent. Such a change probably is not surprising; but that these figures represent, with some qualifications, the proportion living in places of 2,500 inhabitants or more may come as a surprise to you, as it did to me. The Census Bureau has defined "urban" in that one rather limited way since 1900.

Why was I surprised at the way urban was defined by the Census Bureau? To me the concept conjures up a different image than that conveyed by a place having 2,500 inhabitants. "Urban" clearly cannot be defined easily. It is generally thought to be something quite distinct and qualitatively different from "rural." In fact, the emergence of urban society has been viewed as something "revolutionary," to use V. Gordon Childe's term, or as a fundamental transformation of social organization depicted by Adams in *The Evolution of Urban Society* (1966).

The concept of urban is richly differentiated in the writings of urban sociologists with overtones that are not easily captured. I shall try here to give only a flavor of the definitions to give you some idea of what might be lost as one moves from the concept to the concrete problem of measuring it.

That population size has something to do with urban is obvious. Most social scientists, however, would not see size per se as the essential component. Rather, they view the urban concept as defined in terms of some distinctive social institutions and "a way of life," to use Wirth's phrase, that grows out of those distinctive social institutions. The view that "urban" is more properly defined in terms of a distinctive way of life than as a physical or geographical entity predominated in the Chicago School of urban sociology. To quote Robert Park (Park and Burgess 1967):

> The city . . . is something more than a congeries of individual men and of social conveniences—streets, buildings, electrical lights, tramways, and telephones; something more, also, than a mere constellation of institutions and administrative devices— courts, hospitals, school, police, and civil functionaries of various sorts. The city is, rather, a state of mind, a body of customs and traditions, and of the organized attitudes and sentiments that inhere in these customs and are transmitted with this tradition. The city is not, in other words, merely a physical mechanism and an artificial construction. [P. 1]

One characteristic of urban life that is commonly noted is a division of labor and the emergence of vocational specialization. One's occupation becomes a primary organizing principle in life. While the division of labor is bound up with important aspects of the economic and spatial organization of cities, urban sociologists point to its consequences for the moral order of cities, an essential part of the distinctively urban social relations. In particular, they point to bonds of association based on mutual interest rather than on contiguity, personal friendships, and similarity. Human relations in the city are thought to be impersonal and rational, defined in terms of self-interest and the cash nexus. In the view of the urban sociologist there is a substitution of indirect or secondary relations for primary face-to-face relations that characterize the nonurban community. This is not to say that primary relations and relationships based on sentiment rather than mutual interest are totally absent from city life, but rather that the result is something qualitatively different from life in a nonurban or "rural" setting.

Along with these changes in the character of social relationships comes a problem of social control. As Park (Park and Burgess 1967, p. 28) notes, "Control that was formerly based on mores is replaced by control based on positive law." A complex system of political organization, laws, police, courts, administrative regulations, etc., arise to order the relations among individuals and groups and provide the mechanisms of social control. Information transfer, which in nonurban settings is handled by word-of-mouth and gossip, is also transformed by the growth of newspapers, magazines, radio, and television.

One also associates the idea of the city with greater freedom and individuality, characteristics that go along with the greater differentiation and specialization of activities in the city and the decline of social control through public opinion and social ostracism. *Stadt Luft macht frei* refers not only to the freeing of the city dweller from the obligations of the feudal community, but also metaphorically to the city dweller's freedom from the prejudices and conformity pressures of the small-town inhabitant. The freedom of the spirit in the city allows for and encourages the development of individual talents, the flowering of creativity as well as eccentricity. It also has its dark side. As Simmel (1971, p. 334) observes, "It is obviously only the obverse of this freedom that, under certain circumstances, one never feels as lonely and as deserted as in this metropolitan crush of persons. For here, as elsewhere, it is by no means necessary that the freedom of man reflect itself in his emotional life only as a pleasant experience."

How are we to capture such a complex and richly textured concept of urban, of the city, with statistics? If we are to say things about changes in urban life or comparative things about the degree to which different societies are urbanized, we must have some operational definition of what we mean by urban, however imperfect it may be as a reflection of the concept we are talking about. Further, it must be a definition that is capable of being put into effect by the means at the disposal of those responsible for compiling official statistics, such as the Census Bureau, the Bureau of Labor Statistics, or the Department of Agriculture. In the nature of the case it must be something that is unambiguous and not too difficult to carry out.

One of the first scholars to wrestle with the problem of how to measure the change in urbanization was Adna Weber. In his book, *The Growth of Cities in the Nineteenth Century*, published in 1899, he confronted the problem squarely: "When does a dwelling centre cease to be rural and become urban?" he asked.

In ancient times the distinction between city and country, urban and rural, was easily drawn because there were only a few large cities in which life was organized in the ways that we think of as distinctively urban, and these were set off from the surrounding countryside by walls. Weber noted that in addition there were legal distinctions that conferred special rights on cities. In such societies there was not much in the way of a definitional problem. One could easily tell urban from rural.

Weber argued that while the process began earlier in many places it was primarily during the nineteenth century that the sharp distinction between city and country began to break down. How can one differentiate urban from rural? Weber pointed out that size of population is not reliable. Two areas of the same size may have very different patterns of habitation. In one the population may be scattered more or less evenly over the land area, while in the other the population could be concentrated in one small part of the area. Thus, one needs to consider something about the agglomeration of the population.

European statisticians seemed to favor agglomeration as the principle defining feature of urban. For a time in the nineteenth century the average distances between houses was given in the British censuses. But this measure was never adopted by the American census, which, on the whole, tended to use city size as the urban criterion. Weber criticizes the agglomeration notion as a single criterion on the ground that absolute size is also a part of the concept. He notes, for example, that the European land use pattern, in which three hundred people live close together in a village and go out of it to work in their fields, is not much different from the American pattern in which three hundred farmers live on separate farms with houses about a half mile apart, at least not enough different to conform to our notions of the difference between urban and rural.

While recognizing the difficulty in setting precise-size criteria for cities that are applicable between countries or even for the same country over long periods in which the population has grown substantially, Weber argued forcefully for city size as the best simple measures of the concept of urban:

> It is not altogether easy to define the distinguishing characteristics of a city, but in a general way the student will observe that, when a community attains a certain size, new needs and

purposes manifest themselves. The close association of a large body of people alters even the material conditions of life. The artesian well and cistern must give way to a common water supply brought from distant springs; a sewerage system must be introduced, likewise street lighting, and rapid transit between the home and the workshop. The liberty of the individual to do his own sweet pleasure must be curtailed for the common benefit; the streets may not be used as depositories of materials for new buildings; noises must be abated, such as music practice with open windows during the sleeping hours, nuisances are prohibited and the like.... Not only are new wants to be satisfied, but they must be satisfied by new methods. In the country village, where every citizen knows every other citizen, the town meeting, or primary assembly in its pure form, is the ideal governing body, but with every increase in size of the town, representation must be given fuller play. Officials are multiplied by the score and hundred, and must be appointed rather than elected, since the voters are unable to inform themselves concerning the merits of so many candidates. [Pp. 11–12]

What, then, is the size at which "new needs and purposes manifest themselves"? On this question, as with so many among social scientists, there is no agreement. In 1887 the International Statistical Institute adopted a population of 2,000 as the dividing line between city and country. In 1870 the U.S. Census was counting the urban population as that living in cities and towns having at least 8,000 population. After the twelfth census in 1900, this criterion was changed to 2,500 inhabitants. In other countries, a population of 10,000 was regarded as the minimum.

Whether one accepts a lower limit of 2,000, 8,000 or 10,000, it is evident that there are important differences between small and large cities and between towns and cities. Most official statistics in the nineteenth century recognized some sort of distinction among urban population groupings. Even the 1887 report of the International Statistical Institute recognized a category of "great city," with a population over 100,000. Weber himself regarded agglomerations of less than 10,000 as rural, but he divided the rural population into towns (2,000–10,000), hamlet or villages (less than 2,000), and scattered areas. The urban population consists of those living in cities of more than 10,000 population. Great cities are defined as those with populations of more than 100,000.

Deciding on a numerical boundary separating the urban and

rural populations is only part of the problem. What is the unit within which the population is counted? Even in the nineteenth century, defining the unit was not easy. Typically, in the United States, the unit was the political unit, the incorporated village or city, although in New England it was the township, because there were no other incorporated units other than the city. This difference in definition makes comparability of statistics on the urban population difficult.

As cities grew, they began to bump up against neighboring cities or incorporated villages so that there were no intervening rural areas. Statistics that reported only city size failed to capture important differences between the simple size of the city and the economic and social implications of agglomerations of cities and nonpolitical units surrounding many large cities. The concepts of metropolitan counties and districts were introduced sometime after the turn of the century. The "standard metropolitan statistical area" (SMSA) was introduced in the 1950 census to give a better picture of the growth of large urban areas. The standardization of the criteria for defining a metropolitan area went far in the direction of getting statistics collected and reported on a comparable basis, although inevitably there are some deviations and changes in the criteria over time.

The definition of a SMSA is based on counties (except again in New England). Each SMSA contains at least one city with a population of 50,000 or more and an entire county containing that city. In addition it may contain other contiguous counties not containing a city with a population of 50,000 or more that meet specified criteria linking the population of those counties to the large central city of the neighboring county. These subsidiary criteria involve such things as commuting patterns and the proportion of the work force employed in nonagricultural work. They are based on the underlying concept of an integrated economic area with a large volume of daily travel and communication between a central city and its outlying dependent areas. The definition is one that is based on functional relationships that are only partially reflective of the concept of urban as a state of mind.

Since the definition of the SMSA is based on counties, it is apparent that many residents of SMSAs will not be living in cities, even using the small-size criterion. Indeed, in some SMSAs there are rural areas that fit any definition of the term. Thus data on the population of SMSAs would not give us very good data on the proportion of the population living in an urban environment. There is particular ambiguity with regard to those living on the "urban fringe," where housing developments of an essentially urban character may be intermixed with farm land, or villages may be relatively unrelated to a central city in the same county that forms the core of an SMSA.

In order to measure better the urban and rural populations living near large cities, the Bureau of the Census also classifies people as living in urbanized areas (UA) or nonurbanized areas. I would argue that the measure of urbanized area is more closely related to the social scientists' definition of urban, relating to social institutions and a state of mind rather than the quantitative assessments of population density.

Let us look more closely at the criteria for an urbanized area. The definition combines city size and density criteria and attempts to deal with the problems of unincorporated areas and cities which have extended their boundaries to include essentially rural areas, such as those that have consolidated city and county governments. The urbanized area population consists of those people living in areas defined as:

1. Cities of 50,000 inhabitants or more
2. Cities of at least 25,000 inhabitants which, together with those contiguous places (incorporated or unincorporated) with population densities of at least 1,000 persons per square mile, have a combined population of at least 50,000 and constitute for general economic and social purposes a single community, provided that the city is located within an SMSA
3. Territory contiguous to central cities meeting the urbanized criteria that also meet the following criteria:
   a) Incorporated places of 2,500 inhabitants or more but excluding the rural portions of extended cities
   b) Incorporated places with fewer than 2,500 inhabitants, provided that each has a closely settled area of 100 housing units or more
   c) Contiguous small parcels of unincorporated land determined to have a population density of 1,000 inhabitants or more per square mile; areas of large nonresidential tracts devoted to such urban land uses as railroad yards, airports, factories, parks, golf courses,

and cemetaries are excluded in computing the population density

d) A few other small areas of unincorporated territory
without regard to population density in order to eliminate enclaves or narrow fingers of rural areas

Notice that there is a commendable effort made in this definition to deal with the ambiguities of the small areas contiguous
with larger ones and separate those which more nearly conform to
our notion of urban from those that do not. Thus we have elements of density, minimum absolute number of housing units in
close proximity, and the nature of the land use all playing a role in
determining what belongs to an urbanized area.

Our intuitive notions of what constitutes urban may change
over time, and these changes are reflected in the changing rules
for determining what is urban. We have seen that in 1870 the
urban population was simply defined as the population of cities or
towns having at least 8,000 inhabitants. Thirty years later the
criterion was changed to include basically those places having
2,500 or more inhabitants. In 1950 provision was made for reporting statistics on larger urbanized areas, recognizing that these
areas have some distinctive economic and social character that
sets them off from the smaller cities and towns.

The basic image of an urban area that underlies our current
measurement of urbanized areas appears to be a core area with a
population of at least 50,000 plus surrounding areas that meet the
combined density/size criteria. But our ideas about urban density
have also changed somewhat, perhaps as a consequence of the
growth of relatively low-density suburban housing after World
War II. For example, in the 1950 definition of urbanized area the
density criterion for the places less than 2,500 was five hundred or
more units per square mile, a density representing approximately
2,000 persons per square mile and "being normally the minimum
found associated with a closely spaced street pattern." Currently
thes criterion is 1,000 per square mile. This change is not really a
50 percent reduction in the level of density associated with the
idea of urban because average household size has also decreased,
but it does represent a substantial change in our ideas of levels of
density associated with urbanized living patterns.

How well does this definition of urbanized areas meet our intuitive notions of urban? Applying these criteria to the United

States, we find that in 1970 nearly 60 percent of the U.S. population were living in urbanized areas and their central cities. These 275 urbanized areas covered only 1 percent of the total land area of the United States. The average density for the central cities was 4,399 per square mile and 2,589 per square mile for the fringe areas. The average density for the nonurbanized areas was twenty-four persons per square mile. Vermont and Wyoming have no urbanized areas.

Closer to home, we find that, in Indiana, Ogden Dunes and Chesterton are part of the Chicago–Northwestern Indiana urbanized area, while Dune Acres, Beverly Shores, and LaPorte are not. In Illinois, Palos Park is in the urbanized area, Lemont is not. Lake Bluff and Lake Forest are in, Libertyville and Mundelein are not. (For details, see U.S. Bureau of the Census, 1979.)

Twenty-five of the 275 urbanized areas have populations in excess of 1,000,000; fifty-one have populations of less than 75,000. In Texas, Dallas is an urbanized area, so is Harlingen-San Benito. Both Milwaukee and Oshkosh in Wisconsin are urbanized areas.

No set of measurement criteria is apt to satisfy everyone or be useful for all purposes. More important, the consistent application of measures that appear to be fairly adequate reflections of our intuitive notions may produce results that are considerably different from the images we have of the concepts we are using. Thus I expect that when social scientists are doing research on urban life they are more likely to be working in Chicago or St. Louis than in Pine Bluff, Arkansas, or in Owensboro, Kentucky. When I think of classics in urban sociology, I do not usually think of *Middletown*, although Muncie, Indiana, is by no means the smallest urbanized area. When I read that 73.5 percent of the population in 1970 was urban, I do not automatically think of those living in places with 2,500 inhabitants or more. Something has been lost on the way from our concepts to our measures.

Part of the problem, I believe, stems from blending conceptualizations of an urban society distinct from a folk society with conceptions that try to differentiate the peculiar urban character of the "great city" from that of small towns and villages. Anthropologists and other social scientists concerned with the emergence of cities as distinctive forms of social organization concentrate on aspects of urban life that differ from concerns of sociologists and others interested in what differentiates great cities from smaller ones. For one set of concerns, towns of 2,500 may well be different enough from rural areas to qualify for the appelation "urban." When the Secretary of the Department of HUD speaks of urban problems, the term "urban" may imply large cities on the order of 100,000 inhabitants recognized by the 1887 report of the International Statistical Institute as the criterion for a "great city." Probably no set of criteria for measuring the urban population will serve well for all types of inquiry into urban life.

I have discussed here the measurement of only one set of concepts. However, one can easily see that the same types of problems arise with regard to many other terms widely used in the social sciences—unemployment, integration, intelligence, mental health, to name but a few. All have commonsense meanings as well as scientific usages; all have measurement problems associated with them. Many are not as well measured as urban and rural, but the fact that we do not have measures as precise and accepted as those of length, volume, or temperature does not lead me to despair. There is a healthy dialectic going back and forth between attempts to measure concepts and attempts to clarify the meaning of concepts. Measurement attempts often point up ambiguities in definitions that can be resolved. Clarifications of conceptual meaning can lead to better measurement.

The problem is not so much that we lack really good measures of our concepts, but rather that we as investigators or we as people concerned with social policy do not always understand clearly enough how a concept is being measured so that we are misled in the inferences we draw from our measurements. We must all be sure that when we use social statistics we understand fully the way in which the concepts we use are measured and that we do not attribute to them meanings that are not there.

REFERENCES

Adams, Robert McC. *The Evolution of Urban Society*. Chicago: Aldine Publishing Co., 1966
Park, Robert E., and Burgess, Ernest W. *The City*. Chicago: University of Chicago Press, 1967. (Originally published 1925.)
Simmel, Georg. *On Individuality and Social Forms: Selected*

Writings. Edited by Donald N. Levine. (Chicago: University of Chicago Press, 1971.

U.S. Bureau of the Census. *Historical Statistics of the United States: Colonial Times to 1970*. Bicentennial Ed. pt. I. Washington, D.C.: Government Printing Office, 1974.

U.S. Bureau of the Census. "Population and Land Area of Urbanized Areas for the U.S.: 1970 and 1960." *Supplementary Report*. 1970 Census of Population, Series PC (S1)-108. Washington, D.C.: Government Printing Office, 1979.

Weber, Adna F. *The Growth of Cities in the Nineteenth Century: A Study in Statistics*. New York: Macmillan Co., 1899.

Wirth, Louis, ed. *Eleven Twenty-Six: A Decade of Social Science Research*. Chicago: University of Chicago Press, 1940.

12 The Impact of the Polls on National Leadership

Philip E. Converse
UNIVERSITY OF MICHIGAN

My concern today is indeed, as advertised, with the impact of public opinion polling on our national political leadership and with some of the problems which seem to surround this impact. But I would like to address quite broadly the current nature of the processes which in greater or lesser degree link public inputs in the form of poll data to national policy formation, as well as the role which basic social science and social science measurement must play in those processes.

Overarching all of my comments will be the fundamental and abiding normative question as to how much input, and how much control over major decisions, the public at large *should* have. We lack time for any real development of so large a topic. However, as it will hover over everything I say, I should begin by sketching out a hasty frame for any discussion.

Let us place at the radical-democratic pole of the continuum those who believe that the only normative justification for all of the intervening layers of political representation in most modern democracies stem from the simple physical impossibility of packing 100 million adults into Soldiers Field for a town meeting of the whole. This is, according to this extreme view, how it *should* be done. And given the physical impossibility of that, elected representatives are obligated to follow as faithfully as possible the instructions of their constituents.

The opposing pole is often seen to have reached its most eloquent expression in Edmund Burke's speech to the electors of Bristol two centuries ago. It would take a dismal caricature of Burke's thought to locate him all the way to the opposing pole. Burke did not counsel the representative to ignore his constituency. In fact, he assumed that a good representative would keep the interest of his constituents much in view. But he made a sharp distinction between their true interest, as opposed to their

149

momentary expression of will, which is the most that cynics would grant an opinion poll could measure. And the good representative must use his wisdom and judgment to discern when their will and their interest failed to coincide.

If I can discard important nuances left and right, one main issue for Burke was "who's got the expertise." He had no trouble assuming the representative was likely to have it in larger degree than his common constituents. He reviewed the functions of a deliberative body—the information gathering and the many hours spent ventilating different perspectives. Would it not be silly, he asked in one of his more compelling passages, if after all this effort and exposure the representative was expected to vote willy-nilly the instructions of his constituents who had not been exposed to the expertise-sorting experience? And indeed, cast in these terms, it *would* be silly.

If I have described an important continuum of views here, it is one on which persons of equal good will differ, and often dramatically. One group is of particular interest to locate on this continuum. You may recall that founding fathers of survey research and opinion polling in the 1930s were persons of profound democratic convictions. George Gallup, Arch Crosley, Harry Field at NORC, Rensis Likert in the Department of Agriculture, along with various facilitators in the background like Harold Gosnell here and Henry Wallace in Washington—all of these people lay very far toward our most democratic pole.

For them, the combination of population sampling with survey interviewing was not just a methodological development. It was a major political breakthrough. It could remove the chief barrier to true democracy and thereby assure that the voice of the people would be heard in the land.

And this was no mere vested interest on their parts: several of these founding fathers were excited by the political applications well before it was clear that surveys might be a paying proposition. Moreover, in the late 1950s and early 1960s, when the advent of computer networks began to create possibilities of push-botton democracy where all could vote on everything instantaneously from their homes, those of the remaining founders who commented at all were equally enthusiastic, even though such a development had the potential to run them out of business.

At the outset, practicing politicians responded to the new opin-

ion polling with somewhat less enthusiasm. For one thing, representatives sent to Washington had long enjoyed a modest monop-
oly on an understanding of the political pulse within their districts, states, and regions. This was, after all, one of their main
jobs. It was insulting to be told what the opinions of your constituents were, especially by analysts who had never set personal
foot in your district.

There were other suspicions as well. The politician might well
feel that those statistician fellows were earnest enough and
seemed to know what they were talking about. But it was a good
idea to keep your hand on your wallet, because they were also up
to claiming that you could talk to a couple thousand people and
know what 75 million people thought. Anybody could tell that had
to be wrong.

Needless to say, times have changed. Politician suspicion
about the polls has not totally evaporated, thank goodness, but it
surely has subsided on a broad front. Polls are read avidly. Few
national-level politicians care any longer to run a campaign without at least some polling; and the large and well-heeled political
camps all have their own pollsters laureate. Some politicians
understand a certain amount of sampling theory, although we
need not overstate that. Most have at least been indoctrinated
into the magic ±3 percent: if the difference is more than 3 percent
you believe it; if not, you don't.

To say that politicians read polls avidly is not to imply that they
are seeking instructions to follow slavishly. Indeed, the proto-
typic use by political leaders is to learn where more public
relations/cum leadership is needed to win support for what the
leader had in mind doing anyway. Poll information is sought in
hopes of gaining competitive advantage: to be alerted to soft
pedal some unpopular policy thrust over here, or to accentuate
positions that seem to be riding with the tide, and to do so more
agilely than one's opponents.

Indeed, one answer frequently made to those concerned about
limits on relevant expertise in the population, although not an
answer that the most radical democrats are happy with, is that
such poll data have little binding effect in any event. They are
naturally only advisory, not determining. Nonetheless, this new
stream of information, which had no true counterpart a hundred
or even fifty years ago, is inevitably an additional force in the

field. It is bound to exert a shaping influence which is new, and now and again the sense of even more direct cuing seems plain.

The fact of the matter is that in any democratic system there is supposed to be some communication from bottom up as well as the inevitable communication from top down. For some obervers, as for Burke, periodic elections are quite sufficient mechanisms for communication upward. Elections are not just advisory messages: they are legally determining. For other observers, however, elections are quite inadequate by themselves. For one thing, they are rather infrequent. For another, since the vote is usually for people, not policies, the substantive mandate they convey is diffuse. Polls have the potential to be much more timely and much more precisely targeted in policy terms.

It is difficult, as it seems to me, to be averse *on principle alone* to this new river of information, particularly if it is extralegal and advisory. It is equally difficult for me to imagine how this tide might in fact be stemmed, and the waters dried up, even if one wished to do so, which many of us would not. Nonetheless, we know that in practice communication systems are subject to all kinds of pathologies, especially systems as "shaggy" in their contours as this one is at the moment. A reasonable obligation for serious social science is to try to make the kinds of inputs that will help keep these waters as clear and unmuddied as possible.

One of the small inputs that social science has tried to make to polling in the past thirty years is addressed precisely to the question of expertise on the public side of the interaction. The problem is complex. Some discernible fraction of the population will have considerable familiarity with given problem areas, while other fractions will have almost none at all. Much of the population will lie vaguely in between. Sorting all this out in a compelling way is extremely difficult, although it seems worth knowing whether viewpoints differ at different levels of familiarity.

Polling agencies are somewhat more likely to modify opinion with information assessments today than thirty years ago, although it is still not routine. Techniques have even been experimented with to educate respondents in some detail about policy options and their implications before attitudes are elicited, although such procedures are not popular because it is hard to present information without unduly slanting the responses, and in any event the primary interest is in gauging opinion as it exists in its natural state. Probes to assess respondent information on the subject at hand are themselves usually scanty and at times, as we shall see, misleading. The reasons why more adequate assessment of information levels is not carried out has less to do with investigator indifference than with the preciousness of time in an interview: each information probe appended to a policy attitude item serves as a multiplier which is quite frightening, given the usual desire to cover a multiplicity of policy areas in each interview. Nonetheless, the presence of such information modifiers is always welcome.

Watching these opinion-by-information reports casually over the years, I have been impressed mainly at how infrequently major differences open up in opinion across information levels. Nonetheless, marked differences sometimes occur, and it is worth being aware of them.

One of the earlier couplings of opinion and information that caught my eye was drawn in the period of excitement upon the American discovery that the Berlin wall was being built. A national sample was asked to choose among a set of policy options, one of which was for the U.S. to unleash direct military action in Berlin. This option turned out to be a popular one, although it also turned out that much of the enthusiastic endorsement of military action came from respondents who did not happen to know that Berlin was encircled by hostile troops. Cases like this are surely what cause shudders when schemes for push-button democracy are advocated.

Having baited you with this kind of case, however, let me keep you loose with some countervailing ones. It is hard to argue against expertise in an academic setting—it is like being for sin, and I am not up to that. But what gets called expertise has its problems. One of the chief problems is that there is so much of it. Chains of expertise hinged on discrepant premises, both factual and value, and operating at a great many levels of discourse, often stretch as far as the eye can see. They frequently have conflicting bottom lines, or policy implications, which is what brings them into the political arena in the first place.

Given the short time frames which harass policy formation, along with all of the other limitations that Herbert Simon has made famous, such vast potpourris must be selected from. We select toward some chains of expertise and away from others, normally homogenizing the bottom lines in the process.

Let me deal with an example or two. One famous dictum that

dominated American thought for a substantial period was that under no circumstance should the United States let itself become involved in a land war in Asia. This was not a simple one-liner etched on a Mosaic tablet in some wilderness. It was the convergent conclusion of a great many chains of military and geopolitical expertise. It was vigorously selected away from, some time back, for reasons that now seem tragic.

Other bodies of expertise were selected toward, and away from, in the general episode we call Vietnam. At the time of the first teach-in at the University of Michigan, the State Department sent a deputation, after the manner of a Truth Squad, to participate. These deputies patiently explained that if the audience had been privy to documents available in Washington they would understand that the projected involvement would inevitably be brief: "The boys would be home for Christmas." Christmas 1965, that is. When pressed as to what documents gave that impression, it was discovered that they were classified. All that could be said was that they were direct from the field and represented immediate hands-on experience there. This was expertise and taken as preemptive.

Some of you may recall that ten years before the teach-in, in the aftermath of the French defeat in Indo-China, there had been searching postmortems in France as to what had gone wrong. One of the main lessons learned was that all sorts of guiding decisions had been irrelevant or worse, because the field command reports on which they had been based were at such gross discrepancy with the actual situation. The discrepancies were at points so blatant and biased that stray calls for punitive action were heard, although they largely faded as so much spilt milk.

Some of you may recall also that ten years after the teach-in, in the aftermath of the U.S. evacuation from Vietnam, there were again searching postmortems as to what had gone wrong. One of the main lessons learned was that all sorts of guiding decisions had been irrelevant or worse, because the field command reports on which they had been based were at such gross discrepancy with the actual situation. The discrepancies were at points so blatant and biased that stray calls for punitive action were heard, although they largely faded as so much spilt milk.

In short, there is expertise and there is expertise. While it is reasonable to be concerned about decisions controlled from near-total ignorance of situation parameters, there is good cause to respect any reasonably informed opinion, since the name of the game is fully as much selection as possession.

Moreover—and this is scarcely a trivial point—many policy programs will operate well or poorly according to their level of acceptance among the governed. A program which looks technocratically optimal, but which is perceived as unfair or oppressive by the governed, may work out in practice much more poorly than a "suboptimal" version which commands wider respect, support, and cooperation. Resistance can exact a high administrative price. Another important function of the bottom-up communication flow is to provide information as to likely support.

For all these reasons, along with many others, the advent of a more finely tuned communication system is hard to reject in principle, even for those most concerned about expertise.

We might never agree here on the normative issue. But we might agree that if we are to have such a communication system at all, let us at least make it an effective one. The sine qua non of a communication system is that the message as received at the far end of the system has some tolerable relationship to the message as sent at the front end. If what is ultimately decoded bears no relationship to what was encoded, then the system is worse than useless, since it costs money and we might act on what we think we have learned, when we have learned nothing.

Now all communication systems suffer one degree or another of noise. In the ideal case the noise level is calculable, at least as an expected value. In the polling case, the magic 3 percent is a classic example of such a calculation. Unfortunately, it is usually just a beginning. Given the length and shagginess of the intervening communication channel, we must worry about other sources of pure noise as well as sources of signal bias, including the variety of problems which Norman Bradburn and others have examined.

But even this is not all. The tangible message which comes through about a policy matter in an opinion poll is usually disarmingly simple—a set of percentages responding this way or that. If these naked numbers are all we mean by "the message as received," then that is a simple matter. However, I choose the phrase "the message as received" to refer to a good deal more. In the political setting, the numbers taken alone have precious little meaning. They only begin to have action paragraphs as they become freighted with meaning by the receiver. One of the greatest wonders of this business to me is the size of the freight that is usually involved, given the fact that the freighting process is usually so subtle the receiver of the message hardly realizes he is doing it at all. But it is central to the decoding step in the communication system, and here problems can be as rampant as anywhere else.

David Garth, often seen as the shrewdest campaign strategist in the country, has opined that his poll data are no better than anyone else's. He simply knows how to read them better. This is again the message as received, not the numbers taken alone.

An interesting spectacle during the summer of 1978 draws together many of these themes. Elizabeth Drew recounts in the *New Yorker* (1979) the role played by Pat Caddell, the president's pollster, in the sequence of events surrounding President Carter's sudden delay of his major address to the nation, a speech finally given on July 15. Most of the basic themes of the speech, according to Drew, were shaped by Caddell's reading of several batches of poll data. In the wake of the Drew piece, social scientists reviewing the case have concluded that these readings were mistaken.

One major element in the speech was the call to cut oil imports. Hans Zeisel, of the University of Chicago faculty, has done an excellent review of that facet of the speech. Space does not permit rehearsing the details of his argument. Indeed, the complexity of the discussion required to make sober sense of the Caddell data is a lovely example of the size of the freight involved in interpreting such messages. But Zeisel's primary conclusion is: "Caddell's polls seemed to show that cutting oil imports was all the majority of the American people wanted. Careful reading of these polls suggest that they showed nothing of the kind."

A still more central feature of the speech was an effort to restore public confidence. This was prompted by Caddell's discovery that public confidence in government, having declined steadily for more than a decade prior to Carter's election, had taken another precipitous drop in the first two years of his administration. As it turns out, Caddell's indicators of public confidence were largely a subset of items we have used in our

Michigan surveys for many years now. It also turns out that we have independent measurements over the same time span for the Carter administration that Caddell was looking at. They do not show any such drop.

My colleague Warren Miller has published an article (1979) on this discrepancy. One element differing from the Zeisel review is that there is an actual data conflict involved. However, there are major questions of data interpretation in addition. Again, they are too complex to cite, but the question, Miller summarizes, "is whether Carter and Caddell were on target in their conclusions. In my view, they were not." Please remember that the contention here arises on a topic utterly independent of the one discussed by Zeisel, despite the repetition of the dissenting judgment.

I should make clear that the problem here is not unique to Pat Caddell, although we must grant that he has uncommon access to the levers of power. I am convinced that this affliction of the communication process is a much more general one.

One counsel of despair I often hear is that if we cannot get the messages any straighter than this, then let us do without this communication at all. This to me is throwing out the baby with the bath. Some interpretive snarls are much worse than others, and I am selecting bad examples. I feel that there is some coherence and robustness of message underlying most poll results of this kind, if one can take care in ferreting it out. Indeed, I can argue that what is really needed to clarify these messages is often more polls, not fewer.

Let me give a final illustration. Some weeks ago I was contacted by Malcolm Carter of the Associated Press with an intriguing problem in poll interpretation. In April of this year (1979), as SALT II began to move toward the Senate, the major polling agencies went into the field to learn what public sentiment might be toward the treaty. My journalist friend had found published results from a half-dozen major polls, all national, and all conducted within a span of about twelve weeks. He had laid them end to end.

I should like to cast these numbers at you just as they were originally cast at me on the telephone. At first glance they are utterly incoherent, but it is a case where a perfectly intelligible message lies very close to the surface. A casual reader, merely interested in learning the proportion of the population favoring

SALT II, would have found 68 percent favoring it in the first poll. In the second, the figure was 72 percent. In the third it was 33 percent. The next showed 77 percent in favor, the next 34 percent, and the final one 69 percent.

If you are not confused enough yet, two polls broke out results for respondents said to be best informed about SALT. One where the parent sample showed over two-thirds favorable, displayed a figure for the informed rising to 87 percent favorable. The other, starting at one-third favorable only, showed that among the informed public enthusiasm for SALT fell off to a mere 26 percent.

My journalist friend wanted to try out on me what sense he was making of this babel. As he did not put his explanation in my language, I had trouble understanding his point. However, as we sorted percentages, questions, and poll dates more carefully, I began to grasp his deductions, and he was quite right.

Despite the apparent babel, the proportions favorable actually clustered tightly into two groups—one group with two-thirds to three-quarters pro-SALT, the other about one-third pro. Within these groups, the differences looked like garden-variety sampling error. It was between the groups that differences were huge, as though two different questions had been asked. In fact, each question was worded uniquely. But they grouped themselves quite nicely into two types. One type asked about the general desirability of arriving at some kind of strategic arms limitation treaty with the Soviet Union. The other type focused on the specific treaty proposal called SALT II, in one case even rehearsing numerical details about force levels in the question itself. The "in-principle" items drew the large majorities favorable, while the items specifically on SALT II drew only minorities.

What immediately came to mind was an interview I had heard with Senator Baker last summer. He first reviewed all the of the imperative reasons why this country must arrive at a SALT treaty with the Soviet Union, and his bottom line was, "But not this treaty." Senator Baker's position is exactly the difference in the polls.

What about the two so-called informed publics? Again, not too perplexing. For one thing, as you might suspect, the operations defining who was informed on SALT were totally different in the two cases. In one poll, respondents had to volunteer some specifics of SALT II to qualify. These people, keying on the specifics of comparative force levels, were even less enthusiastic about SALT II than their parent populations. In the other case, respondents were deemed "informed" if they could guess which two countries might be trying to come to such a treaty these days. This subgroup was still more favorable to such an arrangement in principle than was its parent population.

Thus the only truly troubling residue in this illustration is that presumably these polling agencies were trying to measure the same thing, and their published reports would leave any casual reader with the impression that they had. The salvation in this instance, as in many others, is precisely the fact that multiple polls were done.

Let me close on two brief and reassuring notes. I always hate to give lavish examples of question-wording oddities because it leaves the impression that any response distribution to a poll item is chiefly determined by what adverbs get thrown in here or there as a question is worded. This simply is not, in general, true. In fact, my colleague Howard Schuman at Michigan has been working for some years in an experimental vein on question wording. He varies wording in deliberately slanted ways trying to produce maximal discrepancies between half samples in order to study these effects systematically. A major frustration has been that with some frequency these comparisons fail to produce discrepancies of workable magnitude. Response distributions seem much more nearly invariant under these transforms than one might suspect. Obviously, occasional thunderous differences do arise, at points which currently seem to remain largely unforeseeable, and we must be on constant guard about them. But this is a far cry from imagining that all results are pure question wording. They are not.

The last cheery note is a postscript to the hortatory cast of my remarks today. I have been saying, in effect, here is a problem which is sobering partly because the political stakes of error can be high. And it is a problem serious social science must do something about. The postscript is that a lot *is* being done about it— vastly more than a decade or two ago—and this attention is increasing rapidly. Several ventures like the Schuman work have been underway for some years, and an assault which is still larger in scale is being organized. A panel is being assembled at the

National Research Council for a general examination of problems of survey research reliability and validity, including topics like conflicting poll results and, hopefully, empirical activities of a new experimental sort. NORC here has been making continuing contributions to that effort, and you will be pleased to know that it will be headed up by another name familiar in these halls—Otis Dudley Duncan.

A first stage will require a far more thorough systematization of difficulties that lie beyond sampling error in these polls than we now possess, so that we will less often be taken by surprise in these matters. A second stage, awesome in itself, will require effective communication of these further traps to readers of poll data, so that the message received will more reliably resemble the message sent.

References

Bradburn, Norman M., and Sudman, Seymour. *Improving Interview Method and Questionnaire Design*. San Francisco: Jossey-Bass, Inc., 1979.

Drew, Elizabeth. "A Reporter at Large." *New Yorker* (August 27, 1979).

Miller, Warrent E. "Misreading the Public Pulse." *Public Opinion*, vol. 2, no. 5 (October–November 1979).

Sudman, S., and Bradburn, N. M. *Response Effects in Surveys: A Review and Synthesis*. Chicago: Aldine Publishing Co., 1974.

Zeisel, Hans. "Lawmaking and Public Opinion Research: The President and Patrick Caddell." *American Bar Foundation Research Journal* (Winter 1980), pp. 133–39.

Index